London Borough of Hounslow

KT-428-391

Hounslow Library Services

020 8570 1028

This item should be returned or renewed by the latest date shown. If it is not required by another reader, you may renew it in person or by telephone (twice only). Please quote your library card number. A charge will be made for items returned or renewed after the date due.

◎ Walking Eye App

YOUR FREE EBOOK AVAILABLE THROUGH THE WALKING EYE APP

Your guide now includes a free eBook to your chosen destination,
for the same great price as before. Simply download the Walking Eye App
from the App Store or Google Play to access your free eBook.

HOW THE WALKING EYE APP WORKS

Through the Walking Eye App, you can purchase a range of eBooks and destination content. However, when you buy this book, you can download the corresponding eBook for free. Just see below in the grey panel where to find your free content and then scan the QR code at the bottom of this page.

Destinations: Download essential destination content featuring recommended sights and attractions, restaurants, hotels and an A–Z of practical information, all available for purchase.

Ships: Interested in ship reviews? Find independent reviews of river and ocean ships in this section, all available for purchase.

eBooks: You can download your free accompanying digital version of this guide here. You will also find a whole range of other eBooks, all available for purchase.

Free access to travel-related blog articles about different destinations, updated on a daily basis.

HOW THE EBOOKS WORK

The eBooks are provided in EPUB file format. Please note that you will need an eBook reader installed on your device to open the file. Many devices come with this as standard, but you may still need to install one manually from Google Play.

The eBook content is identical to the content in the printed guide.

HOW TO DOWNLOAD THE WALKING EYE APP

1. Download the Walking Eye App from the App Store or Google Play.
2. Open the app and select the scanning function from the main menu.
3. Scan the QR code on this page – you will then be asked a security question to verify ownership of the book.
4. Once this has been verified, you will see your eBook in the purchased ebook section, where you will be able to download it.

Other destination apps and eBooks are available for purchase separately or are free with the purchase of the Insight Guide book.

TOP 10 ATTRACTIONS

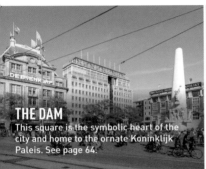

THE DAM
This square is the symbolic heart of the city and home to the ornate Koninklijk Paleis. See page 64.

OUDE KERK
Dating from the early 13th century, it is the oldest church in the city. See page 31.

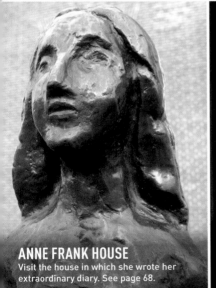

ANNE FRANK HOUSE
Visit the house in which she wrote her extraordinary diary. See page 68.

BEGIJNHOF
Find peace and quiet in the picturesque courtyard, notable for its quaint architecture. See page 62.

A CANAL CRUISE
A leisurely way to see the sights. See page 90.

VAN GOGH MUSEUM
Houses a collection of hundreds of the troubled artist's works. See page 58.

BLOEMENMARKT
Colourful flowers on display all year round. See page 52.

HORTUS BOTANICUS
This botanical garden in the Plantage district houses more than 4,000 species of plants. See page 47.

SCIENCE CENTER NEMO
Get your hands on the latest science and technology in this remarkable ship-shaped museum. See page 51.

RIJKSMUSEUM
Reopened after a 10-year renovation, the city's famous art and history museum is looking better than ever. See page 55.

A PERFECT DAY

9.00am

Breakfast
A leisurely breakfast over the morning newspapers in a grand café, Café Luxembourg, at Spuistraat 24, should hit the spot.

12.00pm

Vondelpark
Continue south to this wild and wonderful park, with its hippie-era history. There is usually plenty of free space amid the trees to escape from the city's hustle and bustle.

10.00am

The Begijnhof
Cross over Spui to the tranquil courtyard garden of this restored medieval *hofje* (almshouse), which was once home to pious single women known as *beguines*, who carried out religious and charitable duties.

11.00am

Leidseplein
Take tram 1, 2 or 5 to Leidseplein, Amsterdam's bustling entertainment square. Maybe fit in a coffee in the spectacular Art Nouveau and Art Deco Café Américain.

1.00pm

Lunch
Vondelpark has three cafés with outdoor terraces and views of greenery but if you want more than a snack join the art crowd at one of the new museum restaurants on Museumplein: the Stedelijk Restaurant in the museum's sleek new extension, or the Rijksmuseum Café in the stunning new atrium. (No admission charge for either.)

4.00pm

Het IJ

Take tram 2 or 5 from Museumplein to Centraal Station, and go to the ferry dock at the rear. Board the free Buiksloterwegveer ferry for a 5-minute trip across the IJ waterway to hip and happening Amsterdam-Noord. Dominating the harbour beside the former Shell tower is the dazzling white EYE Film Institute, a new building with great views from its café.

6.00pm

Anne Frankhuis

Take tram 13, 14 or 17 from Centraal Station to the Westermarkt stop. Waiting times at the Anne Frank House are generally shorter in the evening. On a short visit, stick to the secret rooms where the young diarist, her family and acquaintances spent several years hiding from the Nazis.

2.00pm

Museum fix

Choose between the beautifully restored Rijksmuseum, where the highlights of Holland's Golden Age are a wonder to behold; the Van Gogh Museum, with the world's largest collection of Vincent's paintings or the revamped Stedelijk Museum, dedicated to modern art and design.

8.00pm

Dinner

For an indelibly Amsterdam experience, try De Prins (tel: 020-624 9382), across from the Anne Frank House on Prinsengracht. A good modern Indonesian choice is Kantjil & de Tijger, at Spui 291/3. For an after-dinner drink in a 'brown café', go to Hoppe at Spui 18–20.

CONTENTS

INTRODUCTION

There's no other city on earth like Amsterdam. It is a city of superlatives, having more canals than Venice and more bridges than Paris. It is also one of the prettiest cities in Europe. More than 50 museums – featuring everything from the world's most prominent artists to the history of cannabis – quench the thirst of even the most ardent culture buff, and with 7,000 buildings from the 16th, 17th and 18th centuries, the reflections of its illustrious past happily ripple on into the 21st century. However, the lure of Amsterdam's bricks and mortar is only part of its excitement. Its contemporary culture is vibrant – it's definitely not a city stuck in the past, and its people are open-minded, easy-going and strong-minded, but also down to earth and welcoming to visitors.

Without doubt, though, a major attraction of the city is its historic buildings. The lines of tall, narrow houses with their pretty gables rest beside picture-perfect tree-lined canals. They are connected by humpback bridges and quaint cobbled walkways, which seem to have changed little in nearly 400 years – in fact, since they were walked by the artist Rembrandt and the explorer Abel Tasman, who gave his name to Tasmania.

Amsterdam, which lies in western Holland, close to the North Sea, is a wonderful city to visit. It's small enough to stroll around, and, with the canalside streets too narrow for tour buses, there is no risk of sightseers driving past all the best attractions at high speed. You have to feel the summer sun or see your breath on a crisp winter morning to see what Amsterdam is all about. On a canal tour, the quiet boats allow you to admire the architecture from water level, floating slowly along away from the noise of the modern world.

Water world

Amsterdam contains more than 1,200 bridges crossing more than 100 canals, with a combined length of over 100km (65 miles).

Enjoying one of Amsterdam's many canals

A LIVING CITY

The facades of the buildings may hark back to the past, but the interiors do not. Creative industries, digital hotspots and recycling advice centres, thrive amidst the history. This is no historic ghost town: the city brims with people. Its houses are still lived in (although most are now apartments rather than single-family homes), and its streets are filled with bakeries, delicatessens and wine merchants where people drop in to buy dinner on the way home in the evening. It's all part of the fascinating dichotomy you find at every turn here. The city strides into the future while still holding hands with the past.

The historic heart of Amsterdam has remained relatively unchanged, mainly because of people power. In the latter part of the 20th century, as in most cities, property developers were coveting interesting locations, and in Amsterdam they had their eyes on the old canal houses, knowing they could make a tidy profit by demolishing them and replacing them with something modern. Unfashionable buildings, such as the warehouses of the old docks, were left to the elements. Some Amsterdammers, though, had other ideas. They took to the streets to fight for their city, occupying empty buildings in the warehouse district.

This was typical of the populace, and it wasn't the first time; Amsterdammers have been standing up for what they believe in for centuries. When Protestants were persecuted in the 16th century, they flocked here from all over Europe to take refuge. During World War II, the dockworkers of Amsterdam went on strike in protest against the Nazis' treatment of the Jews in the city. Although in the end the protest was futile, it shows the

AMSTERDAM 'RETURNS' TO THE SEA

The last two decades have seen major new growth along Amsterdam's former docklands. Many of the old harbour installations – wharves, docks, dry docks, warehouses, offices, shipbuilding and ship-repair yards – have either been razed completely or converted to ambitious new projects. Redevelopment of the harbour has afforded vast quantities of space for new housing, cultural, social, entertainment and economic projects, often in leading-edge architectural styles.

Among the highlights east of Centraal Station are the ultramodern Muziekgebouw aan 't IJ concert hall for contemporary music, the adjacent Bimhuis jazz and blues venue and, just inland, the copper-green NEMO Science center, resembling the hulk of a great ship. Along the wharf, seagoing cruise liners berth at the undulating PAT (Passenger Terminal Amsterdam). Offshore, the connected manmade islands Java-Eiland and KNSM-Eiland have been transformed into a contemporary 'city on the water'. Free ferries link Centraal Station with the redeveloped NDSM Wharf, a vast industrial-looking centre, renamed the MediaWharf for its host of creative companies, while just a 3-minute ferry hop across the water from the station, sits the city's sleek EYE Film Institute (see page 90), resembling a spaceship about to take off from the waterfront.

strength of feeling and social awareness that pervades every part of society here.

More than 150 different nationalities live within the city boundaries, a situation that could be fraught with difficulty and strain within a population exceeding 800,000: yet here it has added to the cultural richness built up over centuries of exploration and trade. That doesn't mean to say the city is free from racism, tensions between ethnic groups and concerns about immigration; all of these are perceived to

Amsterdam is the most bicycle-friendly capital city in the world, and has more bicycles than people

have increased since the murder of film-maker Theo van Gogh by an Islamic fundamentalist in 2004.

Amsterdammers seem to have the ability to find creative solutions to their problems. When there wasn't enough housing on the land, they looked at the empty canals and decided that houseboats would help. There are now more than 2,500 on the city's waterways. When cars became a problem in the old town they gave the bicycle priority, and now there are more than 500,000 cycles on the streets – and an estimated 30,000 at the bottom of the canal system at any one time.

Amsterdammers fight for everyone's rights against oppression, or the right of David to stand against the faceless Goliath of bureaucracy. In Amsterdam, when several thousand Davids get together to form a pressure group, Goliath has to sit up and take notice. Amsterdam is a city of 21st-century pressures, such as the problems of traffic and litter – but the problems are faced realistically, debated by the community, and agreed solutions are put into action. When the solutions don't work, the process starts again. It is all seen as a huge learning curve.

Of course, Amsterdam residents don't spend all their time waving protest banners. Many are as industrious and hard-working as their forefathers. They enjoy galleries and exhibitions as much as the visitors do – it can be hard to get tickets because of local demand. And they love to socialise. Bars are popular places in which to meet and put the world to rights. In summer, everyone drinks outside at tables on the streets. Sit down and you may soon be engaged in conversation (most Amsterdammers speak good English).

Amsterdammers enjoy cafés

Amsterdam has many facets, yet they amalgamate into a coherent whole. It is a city of history, which shouts from every gable and corner; a city of culture – of museums, musicians and artists; a city of learning with two large universities; a city of trade with banking at its core; a multi-ethnic city of many different nationalities; a generally tolerant city, in which minority groups may flourish; and a city of tourism, with more than 12 million foreign visitors a year. The beauty of its buildings is undisputed, but it is the sum of all these parts that makes Amsterdam an unforgettable place to visit.

A BRIEF HISTORY

It is difficult to think of a less promising spot for what has become one of the world's major cities. Something must have been appealing about the marshy outlet of the River Amstel where it met the IJ (pronounced 'Aye'), a tidal inlet of the Zuiderzee – even though the area flooded on a regular basis with water forced in by the prevailing winter winds.

The Batavians, a Germanic tribe, travelled down the Rhine to found the first settlements in the river delta around 50bc. The land was entered on maps of the Roman Empire but, following Rome's decline, became the domain of various Germanic tribes in the Dark Ages. This probably had little effect on the settlements, whose main trade was fishing.

FROM FISHING TO TRADING

By around ad 1000, the land we now call the Netherlands was ruled by a number of feudal lords, who had total power over the land and the people who lived on it. The first wooden houses were built on the site of Amsterdam in around ad 1200, on artificial mounds called *terps*. The town was fortified against rival lords and against the seawater, the River Amstel being dammed at what is now the square called the Dam. This was not just to control the tides but also to manipulate trade, as it prevented seagoing ships from taking their goods up the river – they had to transfer the goods to locally owned boats for their journey. It gave the local populace a healthy income and began two important elements in the city's history: the predominance of the merchant classes and the use of barges for inland trade.

In 1275 the settlement of Amstelredamme received permission from Count Floris V of Holland to transport goods on the River Amstel without incurring tolls, giving the city a monopoly on trade along the river. In 1323 Amstelredamme

Het Houten Huys, the oldest house in Amsterdam

became a toll-free port for beer and, once a method of preserving herring had been perfected in the late 14th century, the town also had a product with a high profit margin and began exporting fish around Europe.

The early 15th century saw a healthy expansion of trade, and the population rose dramatically. Catastrophic fires destroyed a large part of the city in 1421 and again in 1452. Following the second fire, legislation made it illegal to build with wood, and brick became the material of choice. Only a few wooden buildings remain from before the 15th-century fires. Het Houten Huys in the Begijnhof is considered to be the oldest. The legislation brought about a feast of civil engineering projects, including the building of the city wall, incorporating the Waag gate and Schreierstoren tower, in c.1480.

THE ARRIVAL OF THE SPANISH

Meanwhile the political climate was changing with a series of dynastic intermarriages. Philip of Burgundy began to bring some semblance of unification to the Low Countries (the region that roughly translates to the Netherlands and Belgium) in the 1420s. He was succeeded by Charles the Bold, whose daughter Maria married into the House of Habsburg. Her son Philip married Isabella of Spain and in 1500 she gave birth to Charles, the future Charles V, ruler of the Netherlands, Holy Roman Emperor, but more importantly, Charles I, king of Spain and all her dominions – an empire on which it was said the sun never set.

Spanish rule was ruthless but, for a while, Amsterdam was left alone. Its position as an important trading post kept it apart from the more barbarous behaviour in other areas. It also saw a threefold increase in its population as refugees flooded in from other parts of the empire. Diamond polishers from Antwerp and Jews from Portugal all brought their influences to the city.

Amsterdam was already developing a reputation for tolerance, as these new and disparate groups settled into the city. At the same time, Martin Luther's new Christian doctrine, Protestantism, was spreading like wildfire across Europe. The teachings of the French Protestant theologian John Calvin took a firm hold in the northern provinces of the Low Countries. It was at this time that Huguenots (French Protestants) came to Amsterdam, fleeing from persecution in their own country.

The Catholic Spanish cracked down on the heretical followers of Calvin, and in 1535 there were anti-papacy demonstrations on the Dam. Strict Catholic leaders took control of the city, and in 1567 Charles V's successor, Philip II, initiated an anti-heresy campaign: Calvinism was outlawed, and repression was ruthless.

TOWARDS INDEPENDENCE

This atmosphere of intense fear and violence sowed the seeds of revolt. The House of Orange (with a power base around the small town of Orange in the south of France) had claim to lands in the Low Countries, and one member, William the Silent, began to organise opposition to Spanish rule. In 1578, the people of Amsterdam rose up against the papal forces and threw them from the city. Unfortunately, though, all thoughts of tolerance were forgotten and the zeal with which the Inquisition sought out Protestants was turned on Catholics. Their churches were violated, and they were forced to convert, or to worship in fearful secrecy. In 1579, seven provinces north of the Rhine concluded the Union of Utrecht, releasing the suffocating grip of Spanish rule. Although William was murdered in 1584, his sons continued his work, and in 1648 the treaties of The Hague and Westphalia organised the northern parts of the Low Countries into the United Provinces.

THE COMING OF THE GOLDEN AGE

As Spanish influence faded, the Dutch star began to rise. First, they drew up agreements with the Portuguese, who had concluded trade treaties in the East that made them the sole source of goods such as spices and silks. Merchants

16th-century map of Amsterdam by Georg Braun and Frans Hogenberg

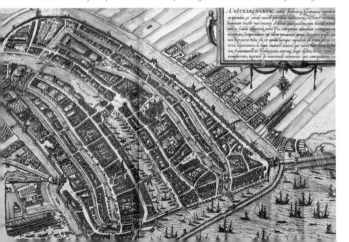

from Amsterdam bought these goods and sold them in the north, making vast profits in the process. When the Spanish took Portugal in 1580, the Amsterdam merchants decided to go into the import business themselves, and in 1595 sent their first fleet to Asia. In 1602 the Vereenigde Oostindische Compagnie (United East India Company, or VOC) was founded in Amsterdam. It obtained a monopoly on all trade routes east of the Cape of Good Hope and secured a monopoly trade agreement with Japan in 1641. VOC ships under the command of Abel Tasman landed in Australia some 150 years before Captain Cook.

Dutch West Indies

The Dutch looked west as well as east, and in 1609 sent Englishman Henry Hudson from Amsterdam to search for a route to China. He traded with the native peoples of Manhattan Island (and named the Hudson River), travelled to the Caribbean, and took several islands as Dutch colonies.

Dutch ships brought back goods not seen before in the Western world: strange and wonderful creatures, new fruits and vegetables, and crafts of great beauty. They were all traded at immense profit with the other nations of Europe as the VOC became more powerful than many countries. Amsterdam and the Netherlands entered the period known as the 'Golden Age'.

Rich merchants needed banks and a financial infrastructure, and these developed quickly in the city. People flooded in to take advantage of the new commercial opportunities, the population rose rapidly, and the old medieval city simply could not cope. It was still contained within the boundaries set almost 150 years before. Plans were made for a series of three new canals – Herengracht, Keizersgracht and Prinsengracht – to form a girdle around the old medieval horseshoe. Canalside lots were sold to the wealthy, who built the finest houses they could afford, but because canal frontage was expensive, the houses were narrow and deep.

The confidence of the city brought opportunities for the burgeoning arts and sciences. The artists Rembrandt, Frans Hals, Vermeer and Paulus Potter were all working in this era, their work much in demand by the merchant classes. At the same time, the Guild of Surgeons was learning about the physiology of the body at their meeting place in the Waag, helped by Antonie van Leeuwenhoek who had invented the microscope.

DECLINE AND FALL

During the 18th century Amsterdam grew into the world's foremost financial centre, but the seeds of decline had already been planted. When the British colonies in New England rose up in revolt against the British, they found ready allies in the Dutch. From their colonies in the Caribbean they sent caches of arms and ammunition. The British were furious and went to war in 1780, destroying the Dutch Navy and precipitating a sudden decline in power and influence from

TULIP MANIA

The first tulips were grown in the Netherlands in 1596 by the botanist Carolus Clusius at the botanical garden of the University of Leiden. These beautiful, colourful flowers were an instant hit – so much so that the first batch of bulbs was stolen. Early in the 17th century, as the economy experienced boom times during Amsterdam's Golden Age, wealthy merchants began to speculate in tulip bulbs, and prices for them rose to ridiculous levels. In 1637 three bulbs changed hands for a price that would have paid for a luxury canalside house. Tulipomania it was called, and it was bound to wither. When suddenly it did, not long after this high point, it drove a number of fortunes into the ground.

which the Netherlands never recovered. Trade suffered to such an extent that in 1791 the VOC went into liquidation.

There were anti-Orange demonstrations by pro-French factions in the country, and in 1795 revolutionary France took the Netherlands. Under the yoke of another foreign power and with trade at an all-time low, the Golden Age was truly over.

William of Orange

THE RETURN OF THE HOUSE OF ORANGE

In 1806, Louis Bonaparte was installed by his brother as king of Holland and chose to make the fine Town Hall on the Dam his palace – now the Koninklijk Paleis. But Louis' secret trade links with Britain and his easygoing attitude to his subjects displeased Napoleon, and in 1810 the emperor forced his brother to abdicate and annexed his kingdom to France. When Napoleon's bubble burst and French power began to wane, William of Orange emerged from exile and was proclaimed king in 1813. Amsterdam had to work its way out of economic decline, but throughout the 19th century the city grew steadily.

Industrialisation changed the city. With the 1889 opening of Centraal Station, built over the old harbour wall, Amsterdam turned its back on its seafaring past and looked forward towards the mechanical age. Some of the oldest canals in the city centre were filled in to allow better access to motorised vehicles. The Dam was landlocked for the first time in its history. However, in the prevailing spirit of the Victorian Age, the philanthropic city fathers funded the building of several major museums and parks, along with instigating social reforms that created what would become one of the first welfare states in the world.

THE 20TH CENTURY

The Netherlands stayed neutral in World War I, and efforts in the first half of the century were concentrated on land reclamation that increased agricultural production and living space. The Zuiderzee was finally tamed with the building of a 30km (19-mile) dyke, the Afsluitdijk, in the north, creating a freshwater lake called the IJsselmeer. During the depression of the early 1930s there were several schemes designed to reduce unemployment, including the creation of the Amsterdamse Bos, a park on the city outskirts.

The Dutch hoped to remain neutral at the outbreak of World War II, but the Germans had other ideas and occupied the Low

The aftermath of a German aerial attack, May 1940

Countries in 1940. Amsterdammers were horrified at the treatment of their Jewish neighbours, and the dockworkers staged a brave one-day strike to protest, but almost all the city's Jews were transported to concentration camps, never to return.

PEOPLE POWER

During the 1960s Amsterdam became a magnet for counter-culture groups such as hippies. 'People power' began to exert its influence, which ensured that progress did not mean sweeping away the past. Where developers saw the opportunity to demolish derelict canal houses and warehouses, the people fought (sometimes literally) to save what they considered their heritage (see page 11). Today much of the historic city is protected by statute, although any redevelopment provokes much debate.

The Netherlands joined the European Union (then the European Economic Community) in 1957. Their natural strengths in agricultural production and trade have ensured their success in the new alliance. The Amsterdam Area has become an important base for foreign companies that have trade ties in Europe. The Dutch have generally been at the forefront of the movement to open national borders, increase people's freedom of movement and expand trade within the EU. Amsterdam has become one of the premier tourist cities in the world, trading on its historic centre and its wealth of artistic collections.

TWENTY-FIRST CENTURY CHALLENGES

As the second decade of the 21st century got underway, some of Amsterdam's cherished multicultural and alternative traditions faced new challenges. The murder of film-maker Theo van Gogh in 2004 for his anti-Muslim views sparked race-relation clashes. In 2010, the inclusion in the coalition government of Geert Wilders did nothing to ease social tensions;

A contemporary apartment block in the Eastern Amsterdam Docklands

the founder of the right wing Party for Freedom (PVV), he is renowned for his criticism of Islam. Amsterdam's renowned liberal attitude to marijuana cafés and prostitution saw a change when city planners announced a clampdown on around 200 window brothels and a third of the hash-smoking coffee shops in the Red Light Quarter.

The Dutch economy – the sixth largest in the eurozone – did not escape the euro crisis. Towards the end of 2013, the Netherlands emerged from its third recession since 2008. A housing bubble has left the Dutch with the highest household-debt levels in the euro zone and house prices have fallen by 20 percent from their peak in 2008. Recently, property prices have gone up again as wealthy foreigners started buying out old houses in the city centre. The gentrification process has affected many neighbourhoods forcing its residents to move out or face a swift rise in cost of living.

To the casual tourist, however, multiracial Amsterdam seems remarkably well integrated and there is little sign of the financial downturn. The city has seen the opening of swish new hotels, Michelin-starred restaurants and luxury designer stores. A billion euros has been spent on the arts in recent years, with new contemporary venues and revamps of galleries including the stunning transformation of the Rijksmuseum. Along the waterfront ambitious new buildings have sprouted in what were formerly derelict docklands.

HISTORICAL LANDMARKS

c.1200 Wooden houses built at mouth of Amstel. The river is dammed.

1275 Count Floris V of Holland grants 'Amstelredamme' the rights to carry cargoes on the river toll-free.

1300 Bishop of Utrecht grants Amsterdam its city charter.

1419 Philip of Burgundy rises to power, unifying the Low Countries.

1452 Fire destroys wooden buildings; new ones to be of brick or stone.

1516 Spain under Charles V rules the Netherlands.

1567 Spain outlaws Calvinism: ruthless repression of Protestants.

1578 The Alteration: Protestants take control of Amsterdam.

1602 United East India Company formed, with HQ in Amsterdam.

1642 Rembrandt paints The Night Watch.

1600–1700 The Golden Age: a Dutch empire built on trade with the East. Canal building in Amsterdam. The arts reach a high point.

1791 The United East India Company goes into liquidation.

1813 The House of Orange returns to power.

1889 Centraal Station opened.

1940 Neutral Netherlands invaded by German forces.

1944–5 The Winter of Hunger.

1960s 'People power' saves parts of historic Amsterdam from redevelopment. Amsterdam becomes home to minority groups.

2004 After making a film critical of Islam, director Theo van Gogh is murdered in Amsterdam.

2005 Muziekgebouw aan 't IJ concert hall opens on the waterfront.

2007 City Council introduces the controversial Project 1012 to reduce cannabis cafés and brothel windows in the Red Light district.

2010 Canal Ring receives Unesco World Heritage Site status.

2013 Abdication of Queen Beatrix of the Netherlands and inauguration of King Willem-Alexander. Rijksmuseum reopens after a decade-long restoration. Minimum legal age for a prostitute is raised from 18 to 21.

2014 Malaysia Airlines Flight MH17 leaves Amsterdam for Kuala Lumpur but is shot down over Ukraine. All 298 people on board are killed.

2016 Amsterdam named the European Capital of Innovation until 2018.

WHERE TO GO

Amsterdam is a small city and eminently walkable, but if you only have a short time, take advantage of the tram system, which can transport you efficiently to all the most important attractions. Perhaps the most disconcerting thing for newcomers is how to find their way around. The centre of Amsterdam can seem at first like a maze of tiny streets and canals with no overall plan. But think of it as a large spider's web, and once you understand the structure of the town, it is relatively easy to get around. The central core, around the square called the Dam, is horseshoe-shaped, and consists of a series of wide streets (the main one is Damrak/Rokin, which cuts right through the centre) and narrow alleys. It also has some of the oldest waterways, once so important for the delivery of goods from around the Dutch trading world.

This area is ringed by a girdle of canals (grachten), the major ones running outward in ever-larger circles. Singel was once the outer barrier for medieval Amstelredamme, but as the city expanded, Herengracht (Gentlemen's Canal), Keizersgracht (Emperor's Canal) and

I amsterdam Card

The VVV (tourist information centre, see page 128) sells the I amsterdam Card, giving free entrance to over 40 museums and attractions, unlimited access to city public transport (GVB) and a free canal cruise. (Note that Rijksmuseum is excluded, although there is a small reduction.) You'll also get discounts on bike hire and some bars and restaurants. A 24-hour card costs €55, a 48-hour card €65, a 72-hour card €75 and a 96-hour card €85 (2016 rates). Cards can also be purchased online at www.iamsterdamcard.com.

A large barge passes under a bridge

Just a few of Amsterdam's half a million bicycles

Prinsengracht (Princes' Canal) enlarged the web. If you ever feel confused when strolling around town, remember that these three canals spread outwards in alphabetical order: H, K and P.

Small streets *(straatjes)* radiate out from the centre, crossing the canals by means of the thousand-plus bridges, which are such a distinctive part of the city landscape. To the north of the city centre, the IJ waterway joins the IJsselmeer (a former inlet of the North Sea, now dammed); west of the IJ is the Noordzeekanaal, Amsterdam's present-day route to the open sea.

This guide divides the city into four sections that are easy to follow on foot. We start in the centre of the city, where you will be able to get your bearings, obtain whatever information you need from the VVV tourist information office (see pages 30 and 128) and take a **canal boat tour** – one of the best ways to get an overview of historic Amsterdam and to admire the city's true beauty (see page 122).

STATIONSPLEIN TO DAMRAK 29

THE CENTRE

Central Amsterdam – once the medieval city – is very small indeed. The port was the lifeblood of the city at that time and ships would sail right into the heart of Amstelredamme, as it was known. Only a few architectural gems are left to remind us of this era, but the tangle of narrow alleyways gives a feel of the hustle and bustle that must have surrounded the traders.

STATIONSPLEIN TO DAMRAK

The decision to locate **Centraal Station** ❶ (www.amsterdam centraal.nu), on the site of the old harbour wall was the final death-knell of maritime trade for the city. It stopped large cargo ships from landing their cargoes and diminished the importance of the canal systems.

The station, opened in 1889, dominates the view up Damrak. The grand building was designed by P.J.H. Cuypers, who was also responsible for the design of the Rijksmuseum, and sits on three artificial islands supported by 8,687 wooden piles. The station has undergone an extensive redevelopment, including a new bus station and platforms that accommodate international high-speed rail services, but work on the controversial North-South metro link (see page 130) is likely to continue until 2018.

LEAN TIMES

As you stroll along the canalsides you will notice that there are very few houses standing absolutely upright – in fact, some seem to lean at a precarious angle. Don't assume that this is because of subsidence; most were designed to tilt towards the canal so that goods could be winched to the upper floors without crashing into the side of the house. Unfortunately, some of them tilted too much, resulting in the 1565 building code, which limited the inclination to 1 in 25.

East of the station, on the redeveloped waterfront north of Piet Heinkade, stands the landmark **Muziekgebouw aan 't IJ** (literally Music Building on the IJ; www.muziek gebouw.nl), focusing on contemporary classical music. Another prominent modern building, close to the station, is the **Centrale Bibliotheek** (built in 2007; www.oba.nl), the largest public library in Europe; with internet terminals galore, study pods and superb views from its excellent 7th floor cafeteria.

Back at **Stationsplein**, in front of Centraal Station, is the **VVV Amsterdam Tourist Office** (see page 128). It is housed in the Noord-Zuid Hollands Koffiehuis, dating from 1919, which was rebuilt in 1981 from the preserved pieces of the original, having been dismantled when the metro was constructed in 1972. You will also find canal tour boats moored here.

Walk across the square towards the city and, on the canal bridge, you will see on your left the distinctive spires of **Sint-Nicolaaskerk** (St Nicholas Church; www.nicolaas-parochie.nl; normally Tue–Fri 11am–4pm, Mon and Sat noon–3pm; free). This Catholic church, completed in 1887, replaced many of the secret chapels that were built for worship during the period of Catholic persecu-

Sint-Nicolaaskerk

tion. Once over the bridge you will be on **Damrak**. Plans are afoot to smarten up this gateway to the city and replace massage parlours and tourist tat with high-end restaurants, hotels and entertainment. At the head of Damrak is the **Beurs van Berlage ②** (Berlage Stock Exchange; www.beursvan

The Gothic Oude Kerk

berlage.nl; guided tours at 11am), the old stock exchange. Its refined modern lines were a revelation when it opened in 1903. Unfortunately, it didn't excite traders and is now used for conferences and events.

OUDE KERK

The warren of streets to the left of the Beurs building is what Amsterdammers call the **Oude Zijde** (Old Side). This was the old warehouse district in medieval times. The narrow alleyways are darker than in the modern parts of the city and the houses are even narrower and taller. Dominating the streets is the imposing Gothic **Oude Kerk** ❸ (Old Church; https://oudekerk.nl; Mon–Sat 11am–6pm, Sun 1–5.30pm).

The Oude Kerk is the oldest parish church in Amsterdam; work began in the early 13th century when Amstelredamme was a new trading town. Over the next three centuries, the church underwent several extensions until it took on the unusual shape it has today, with several chapels adding gables to the original

The Red Light District is one of the liveliest areas after dark

structure. In the early days it acted as a marketplace and a hostel for the poor. Today it hosts concerts and exhibitions.

Inside, the scale of the church is impressive. Commemorative tombstones, including that of Saskia, Rembrandt's wife, cover the floor. The stained-glass windows are glorious. One, commemorating the Peace of Münster, shows a Spanish official handing over the charter recognising the independent Dutch state. Opposite the Oude Kerk, is a step-gabled, Baroque Dutch Renaissance house, **De Gecroonde Raep** (The Crowned Turnip), dating from 1615.

THE RED LIGHT DISTRICT

The northern reaches of the canalside streets Oudezijds Voorburgwal and Oudezijds Achterburgwal, southwest of the Oude Kerk, are home to Amsterdam's infamous **Red Light District**, known as the Wallen (Walls). As in any large port, prostitution has always been rife and, although some Calvinists tried to stamp it out, it still thrives today.

The area is safe (except perhaps in the early hours of the morning) and usually busy with tourists. The tree-lined canals and old, narrow iron bridges are some of the prettiest in the city, and most prostitutes ply their trade behind relatively discreet windows, not on the streets.

At ground level, there are shops – seedy, eye-catching or amusing, depending on your point of view – selling sex wares and attracting customers. But don't get too distracted, or you will miss the rows of dainty gables, quirky wall plaques and window boxes brimming with flowers, which give the whole area a cheery feel. Don't be surprised to find offices, shops and restaurants side by side with the brothels here – it's all part of Amsterdam life. At night the streets come alive with bars, clubs and adult shows and it becomes one of the liveliest parts of the city. Make sure you stay on the busier, well-lit thoroughfares on your way back to your hotel.

SEX AND DRUGS

Amsterdam has been cleaning up its act, clamping down on brothels and cannabis coffee shops and replacing them with higher-end cafés, restaurants, shops and galleries. Project 1012, launched by the city authorities in 2007, is aiming at reducing organised crime, drug-dealing and sex trafficking. But Amsterdam would not be Amsterdam without the bordellos and cannabis cafés so well over half the former and a third of the latter are being retained. Plans are afoot to banish all the bordellos around the incongruously located Oude Kerk (Old Church). Currently it is still overlooked by prostitutes bathed in the light of red lamps but also by the windows of new initiatives such as Red Light Radio (http://redlight radio.net), an online radio station where DJs broadcast from a former bordello.

MUSEUM HET AMSTELKRING

D'Leeuwenburg Huis

You will find several histori-cal gems as you wander the Wallen. One of the narrow houses on Oudezijds Voor-burgwal (No. 40) has a won-derful secret to share. **Ons' Lieve Heer op Solder ❹** (Our Lord in the Attic; www.opsolder.nl; Mon–Sat 10am–5pm, Sun and holidays 1–5pm) was a merchant's house bought by the Catholic Jan Hartman in 1661. Following the 'Alteration' in 1578, Catholics were not permitted to practise their religion, so Hartman, along with a number of other wealthy Catholics of the time, had a secret chapel built for family worship. Although they were common at the time, this is now the only complete secret chapel left in the city. Three additional houses were added to create extra space, and several of the other rooms are furnished in 18th-century style. It is a fascinating glimpse of a difficult time in Amsterdam's history, but it's not just a museum piece – it is still used for weddings. A few doors along from the Amstelkring is the Dutch Renaissance **D'Leeuwenburg Huis**, a restored step-gabled house dating from 1605.

DE WAAG

Southeast of the Oude Kerk you can walk through the small Chinese Quarter to reach **De Waag ❺** (Weigh House). One of the oldest buildings in the city, it opened in 1488 as a city gate to mark the eastern boundary of the city along the new wall built after the disastrous fire in the 1450s. The numerous turrets and rounded tower give it the look of a fairy-tale castle but it has had a more gruesome history. Public executions were held here in the 16th century, with the condemned being kept in a small cell on the ground floor before they met their fate.

From the early 17th century it became the weigh house (waaggebouw) for cargoes entering or leaving the city down the Geldersekade canal to the north. The upper floors were used by trades' guilds for meetings and by the Guild of Surgeons for practical medical research, including experiments with cadavers. Two of Rembrandt's most celebrated paintings, *The Anatomy Lesson of Dr Deijman* and *The Anatomy Lesson of Dr Tulp* were commissioned by the Guild of Surgeons and originally hung in the Waag.

In the early 19th century the weigh house closed, and the Waag had a number of less illustrious tenants. It now houses a superb café-restaurant, called In de Waag (see page 106), so

De Waag is one of the city's oldest buildings

The Schreierstoren

you can stop for refreshment and admire the Gothic interior at the same time.

NIEUWMARKT AND ZUIDERKERK

Despite the name, **Nieuwmarkt** (New Market) celebrated its 400th anniversary in 2015. It surrounds the Waag and is home to several different types of market throughout the week. If you walk to the north side of the Waag and look along Geldersekade you will see a tower dominating the skyline. This is the **Schreierstoren**, which is also part of the new city wall that was constructed in 1480. The tower's name is thought to derive from the word *schreien*, which means 'weeping', as it was a place where sailors' wives came to wave their men off to sea, fearing for their safety. The tower now houses the VOC Café, an attractive old-style bar (www.schreierstoren.nl).

From the Waag, walk down Sint-Antoniesbreestraat, past modern apartment blocks built in the 1970s. Look out for the magnificent **De Pintohuis** (www.huisdepinto.nl) at No. 69, a mansion bought by wealthy Jewish merchant Isaäc de Pinto in 1651, and rebuilt in 1686 by his son David Emanuel, who gave it more or less its present ornate appearance.

Off the right side of Sint-Antoniesbreestraat is the ornate tower of the **Zuiderkerk** ❻ (South Church; http://zuiderkerk amsterdam.nl). Begun in 1603, this was the city's first Protestant place of worship to be built after the Reformation. Designed by Hendrick de Keyser, it was deconsecrated in 1929 and is now rented out for private and corporate events.

At the end of Sint-Antoniesbreestraat is a tiny square with a wonderful view along Oude Schans canal to your left. You will find a crooked little house, dating from the 17th century. Formerly a lockkeeper's house, it is now a small bar/café, De Sluyswacht (www.sluyswacht.nl), set against the backdrop of the canal and **Montelbaanstoren** behind. Built as part of a new outer defensive wall in 1512, the tower originally had a flat roof – the ornate peak that gives it such panache was added by Hendrick de Keyser in 1606.

REMBRANDT'S HOUSE

After pausing to take a photo, cross the street to Jodenbreestraat (Jewish Broad Street) and the three-storey brick building with red shutters. This is the **Museum Het Rembrandthuis** **❼** (Rembrandt House Museum; www.rembrandthuis.nl; daily 10am–6pm; tickets can be purchased online), which was home to

REMBRANDT'S INSPIRATION

Rembrandt van Rijn had a passion for collecting rare or precious objects. This desire played a part in his downfall, but his collection at the Rembrandthuis (see page 37) tells us much about Dutch society in the 1600s. Beautiful man-made items from the Dutch colonies sit beside Roman and Greek sculptures from the Classical era. There are a number of globes, indicating the expansion of the known world in Rembrandt's time, seashells and strange stuffed beasts from far-off lands, and etchings by Raphael, Titian and Holbein, kept in heavy leather-bound books, showing new visual styles in form and colour. Inspiration was rich indeed in 17th-century Amsterdam.

the great artist from 1639 to 1660. Rembrandt bought the house as he rose in prestige and wealth. He created a studio on the top floor, where there was abundant natural light to illuminate his subjects, and sufficient space for him to teach his numerous pupils. The painter lived with his wife, Saskia, and their young son on the first floor. Unfortunately, he was not able to live out his life in his home. His lack of financial acumen and love of expensive objects brought him to bankruptcy in 1656 and he had to sell all his possessions, including the house, in 1660.

The whole house was restored in the late 1990s, including the studio and the painter's *kunstkamer* or art cabinet (see page 37), to re-create the early 1600s as faithfully as possible. The artist's studio, north facing and flooded with light, is wonderfully atmospheric, and the kitchen, with its open fireplace, is always popular with visitors. More than 250 of the artist's etchings are beautifully presented around the upper floors of the house.

The Polders

Some 6,500 sq km (2,500 sq miles) of the Netherlands has been reclaimed from the sea. This was achieved by building dykes along the coast, rivers and canals, and pumping the ground water to the far side of the dyke to dry out the land. The reclaimed tracts of land between the dykes are called polders. Many areas of Amsterdam, such as Vondelpark, are 2m (6.7ft) below sea level, and Schiphol Airport is 4.5m (15ft) below sea level.

THE SOUTHEAST

WATERLOOPLEIN

Parallel to Jodenbreestraat, on its left-hand side, is **Waterlooplein** ❽, named after the famous battle and home to a sprawling flea market of the same name (http://waterlooplein.amster dam). Every day (except Sunday) you'll find an eclectic mix of second-hand crockery, curios and electrical goods on sale, along with ethnic and vintage clothes.

The flea market at Waterlooplein is the oldest in Amsterdam

The eastern end of the market square is dominated by the twin spires of **Mozes en Aäronkerk** (Moses and Aaron Church; www.santegidio.nl/mozes-en-aaronkerk-gewijd), a Catholic church built in 1840 on the site of a secret chapel. The Old Testament figures of Moses and Aaron were found depicted on gable stones in the original building and were set into the wall of the new edifice. The fine towers are actually wood rather than stone. They were painted to match the sandstone walls in a 1990 restoration.

Waterlooplein, and its market, used to be much larger, but a massive building project, begun in the early 1980s, reduced its size considerably. Protesters deplored the loss of several old canal houses fringing the square, which constituted much of what was left of the old Jewish Quarter. In the 1980s squatters battled against riot police and water cannons. Nevertheless, the construction went ahead, and the result of this labour is the conjoined National Opera & Ballet (www.operaballet.nl) and **Stadhuis** (Town Hall), sitting majestically on the River Amstel. Opened in 1986, the attractive glass-fronted home to the Netherlands Opera and the National Ballet hosts a range of travelling companies in the largest auditorium in the country.

At one end of Waterlooplein is the **Joods Verzetmonument**, a black marble memorial commemorating Jewish Resistance fighters from World War II.

TOWARDS MAGERE BRUG

The **River Amstel** has always been a major artery through the city and even today you will see a large amount of commercial traffic passing along the waterway. From the terrace and walkway around the National Opera & Ballet there are wonderful views of the boats and the canal houses bordering the water. The bridge in front of the opera provides a wonderful view down the river and is also one of the most interesting bridges in Amsterdam. The **Blauwbrug** (Blue Bridge) is named after the colour of the previous bridge that occupied the site. The present one, dating from 1880, is based on Pont Alexandre III in Paris and is ornamented with carvings of ships and other maritime themes.

THE SKINNY SISTERS

How did the Magere Brug get its name? *Mager* means 'skinny' in Dutch, and it would be simple to assume that its name refers to the narrowness of the bridge. Not so, say Amsterdammers, who will regale you with stories of two sisters called Mager who each had a house on opposite sides of the bridge and who paid for the original bridge to be built. By amazing coincidence, these two sisters were also thin, which prompts comments about the '*mager* Mager sisters'.

A block upstream from the Blauwbrug on the east (right) bank is the huge neo-classical Amstelhof (1681), a former almshouse for the elderly that is now the site of the **Hermitage Amsterdam** ❾ (www.hermitage.nl; daily 10am–5pm), a branch of St Petersburg's State Hermitage Museum. Spacious modern galleries are the setting for two blockbusters a year, both lasting six months.

Although the Blauwbrug is the most ornate bridge in the city, Amsterdammers and visitors alike have a soft spot for its neighbour a little way south up the Amstel, the

The picturesque Magere Brug

Magere Brug or 'Skinny Bridge'. This white, wooden drawbridge is picture-perfect and one of the most enduring symbols of the city. It is even prettier at dusk when the lights on its arches and spars are switched on. There has been a bridge here since the 1670s but the present one was erected only in 1969.

Along the river on either side of the Magere Brug are a number of old barges moored along the banks. The large craft, which would once have carried heavy cargoes such as grain and coal, now make surprisingly large, comfortable, quirky and very expensive homes. Beyond, on the east bank of the Amstel, you will see the facade of the **Koninklijk Theater Carré** (https://carre.nl). Traditionally the site of the Carré Circus, this was where the Carré family had a wooden building erected to house their shows. Later the authorities deemed this structure to be a fire hazard and so the Carrés had this beautiful stone building designed for them. It opened for performances in 1887 and now hosts many different types of performance throughout the year, but a circus always appears here at Christmas time.

HERENGRACHT

Cross the river via the Magere Brug then travel one block north and take a left along the northern bank of **Herengracht**. Here, you will get your first look at the canal system that was built during Amsterdam's 17th-century Golden Age, revolutionising the city. During its time, this was probably the most sought-after, expensive real estate in the world.

Herengracht has numerous beautiful houses, which can only really be appreciated by strolling past them. This part of town is still mostly residential, and many houses have been converted into apartments for wealthy and successful Amsterdammers. It is fascinating to peek inside at the ultramodern interiors, which give a feel of the flair the Dutch have for interior design.

MUSEUM WILLET-HOLTHUYSEN

At No. 605 Herengracht, the **Museum Willet-Holthuysen** ❿ (www.willetholthuysen.nl; Mon–Fri 10am–5pm, Sat–Sun 11am–5pm) gives you the opportunity to look behind the facade of a genuine Golden Age house. It was completed in 1687 and structurally has changed very little since that time, although it has been altered cosmetically several times as fashions changed.

Watch your step!

Wear comfortable shoes when you explore the city: uneven surfaces can be hard on the feet – especially the cobbled canalside roads, which are made even more irregular by tree roots.

Gentleman's parlour at the Museum Willet-Holthuysen

In 1855 it came into the possession of Gerard Holthuysen, a successful trader in glass and English coal. His daughter married Abraham Willet, a founding member of the Dutch Royal Antiquarian Society, whose aim was to promote national art and history.

On her death in 1895, Louisa bequeathed the house and its contents to the city of Amsterdam on the one condition that it would be opened as a museum. This it duly was in 1896, and today visitors can examine in detail the furniture, porcelain and numerous artworks that had been collected by the Willet-Holthuysen family over many years.

Continue along Herengracht for the **Tassenmuseum** (Museum of Bags and Purses, www.tassenmuseum.nl; daily 10am-5pm), an exquisite collection on three floors of the distinguished canalside home of Amsterdam's mayor in the 1660s. Follow 500 years of bags and purses, from 17th century silver framed pouches, gaming bags and chatelaines through to Art Deco and stylish contemporary

Explore Jewish culture at the Joods Historisch Museum

designs. A pretty garden café offers tempting teas.

REGULIERSGRACHT AND MUSEUM VAN LOON

A short walk brings you to the bridge at Reguliersgracht with one of the most fascinating views of the canal ring. From here it is possible to see 14 other bridges by looking up and down Herengracht and ahead down adjoining Reguliersgracht (this view is even better at water level, so take a canal cruise – and your camera – see page 122). Reguliersgracht has some very pretty houses and is quieter than the main three 'girdle' canals, which were built at the same time. Go south along Reguliersgracht and turn right on the far side of Kiezersgracht. At No. 672 you will find a canalside residence dating from 1672 that houses the **Museum Van Loon** ⑪ (www.museumvanloon.nl; daily 11am–5pm). One of the city's finest canalside mansions it was acquired by descendants of Willem Van Loon, co-founder of the East India Company. The elegant if slightly faded interior includes antiques, rich wallpaper and portraits from generations of the influential Van Loon family. In the ornamental garden (rarely open to the public) there is a coach house in the style of a Greek temple. On the opposite side of the canal the trendy **Foam Fotografiemuseum** (Foam Photography Museum; www.foam.org; Sat–Wed 10am–6pm, Thu–Fri until 9pm) has regularly changing exhibitions featuring famous names as well as emerging young talent.

THORBECKEPLEIN AND REMBRANDTPLEIN

Back at the bridge with the views, the small square to the north is the rather touristy **Thorbeckeplein**, where you will see a sombre statue of Johan Rudolf Thorbecke who designed the Dutch Constitution in 1848. Wander through the square, which is the scene of an art market on Sunday, to reach **Rembrandtplein** **12**, one of the city's most vibrant social centres. This square was formerly called Botermarkt (a butter market was held here in the 19th century), but it was renamed when the large statue of Rembrandt was sited here in 1878.

One wonders what the artist would have made of the square, since it is now busy with theatres, cinemas, clubs, show halls, bars and restaurants – and dominated by vibrant neon signs. On a summer evening, however, it is a wonderful place to sit with a drink and watch the world go by.

An opulent bed at the Museum Van Loon

THE JEWISH QUARTER

Beyond the eastern end of Waterlooplein you will see the Mr Visserplein, busy with several lanes of traffic. Head across the square to Weesperstraat and Jonas Daniël Meijerplein to find the **Joods Historisch Museum** **13** (Jewish Historical Museum;

Exploring the Hortus Botanicus

www.jhm.nl; daily 11am–5pm), which documents the history of the once large and influential Jewish community in the city. Jewish history in Amsterdam dates back to the late 16th century, but was cut short by the Nazi occupation of the city that began in 1940.

The systematic deportation of the Jewish population to concentration camps tore the community apart, and after the war only a handful returned to their homes. The museum, which opened in 1987, was created by the amalgamation of four old Ashkenazi synagogue buildings. The exhibitions reveal the history of Amsterdam's Jewish community, explain the philosophies of Judaism and examine the wider issues of Jewish identity.

Across busy Weesperstraat are two other reminders of the once thriving Jewish community. In a stark, exposed position near the road in Jonas Daniël Meijerplein, is the **Dokwerker Statue** by Mari Andriessen. This figure commemorates the day in February 1941 when the dockworkers rose up in protest against the Nazi deportation of the Jews. Behind the statue is the **Portugese Synagoge**  (www.portugesesynagoge. nl; Sun–Thu Feb–Nov 10am–5pm, Fri May–Sep 10am–5pm, Sep–Oct and Mar–Apr until 4pm, Nov–Feb 10am–2pm), inaugurated in 1675 for the Spanish and Portuguese Sephardic Jews who settled in the city. Its design is said to be based on that of King Solomon's Temple.

THE PLANTAGE

From Jonas Daniël Meijerplein look southeast to the glasshouses of the **Hortus Botanicus**  (Botanical Garden; www.dehortus.nl; daily 10am–5pm, July–Aug Sun until 7pm, free guided tours on Sun), easily seen just across Nieuwe Herengracht. Cross the canal by walking left along its banks to the nearby bridge. Once across, you have entered the Plantage area of the city, formerly an area of parkland but developed from the mid-19th century into one of the first of Amsterdam's suburbs.

The Botanical Garden has a long and illustrious history. It began as a small medicinal garden in 1682, but soon became the depository for many of the new plant species brought from Dutch colonies in the Golden Age, and was responsible for developing each genus for cultivation, propagation and commercial exploitation. The distinctive glasshouses were added in 1912, and today the gardens have one of the largest collections in the world.

The 17th-century Portugese Synagoge

A two-minute walk down Plantage Middenlaan leads you to **Artis** ⓰ (www.artis.nl; March–Oct daily 9am–6pm, Sat Jun–Aug until sunset, Nov–Feb daily 9am–5pm; charge), a fascinating complex of zoo, aquarium, planetarium and geological museum, which aims to increase visitors' knowledge of the physical world. The zoo was one of the first in Europe when it opened its doors in 1838, and it has continued as a groundbreaking institution, now acting as a centre for efforts to save several endangered species. The **Microtopia** (www.micropia.nl; Sun–Wed 9am–6pm, Tue–Sat 9am–8pm) is a unique museum presenting microbes and their presence in human life.

TROPENMUSEUM

Southeast of Artis, across two canals and busy roads, is **Oosterpark**, an open green area with a lake and play areas (take tram No. 9 or 14 rather than walking here from the city centre). In the northern corner of the park is the **Tropenmuseum** ⓱ (Tropical Museum: www.tropenmuseum.nl; Tue–Sun and Mon during public and school holidays 10am–5pm), once the home of the Dutch Colonial Institute. The building was constructed in 1926 to house the institute's

AMSTERDAM STREET ADDRESSES

A formal system of addresses with street names and numbers was only introduced to the city by the French in 1795. Before this, gable stones and wall plaques were used as a way of indicating either the purpose of a commercial building or of explaining the precise site of a home. Directions might have been something like 'three doors down from the Red Fox'. Some of these plaques have been left in place – look out for them as you stroll the banks of the canals.

Exhibits in the Tropenmuseum

collection of artefacts from the tropics. Today, the aim of the museum is to improve our knowledge of the world's tropical areas and promote an understanding of the peoples in these developing parts of the world. A vast collection of artefacts from the former Dutch East Indies (now Indonesia) was the starting point for the displays, which range from tribal masks to tools and utensils. Recreations of a Bombay street and Arab souk, among other locales, bring home the reality of life in different societies. The museum also has an award-winning **Tropenmuseum Junior** (Children's Museum) offering six to 13 year-olds a chance to explore the collection and interact with the exhibits.

ENTREPOTDOK

North of Artis is **Entrepotdok**, which, in the 19th century, was the warehouse region of the city, with carefully designed canals forming one of the busiest port areas in Europe. The warehouses fell into disrepair in the 20th century and lay empty for many years before they became a centre for the 1960s' and 1970s' squatter revolution that overtook the city. Since the 1980s, the area has been totally renovated and the warehouses gutted to create spacious modern housing, offices, and bars and restaurants without changing the basic design of the buildings.

Heading north, you will reach the main street, Prins Hendrikkade, which takes you back to Centraal Station, to the left. As you cross over the Nieuwe Vaart canal, look left for a glimpse of the only windmill left in the city's central area. The **De Gooyer windmill** (www.molens.nl) was built in the early 18th century to grind corn. It sits next to a small brewery, Brouwerij't IJ (www.brouwerijhetij.nl), which has guided tours and tastings, and a bar with an outdoor terrace.

THE HET SCHEEPVAARTMUSEUM

Across the bridge, walk towards Kattenburgerplein and a large square building housing the **Het Scheepvaartmuseum** ⓭ (Maritime Museum; www.hetscheepvaartmuseum.nl; daily 9am–5pm). This building was constructed in 1656 for the Navy, and its strong walls safeguarded a vast arsenal that once protected Dutch interests around the world. The museum has been beautifully renovated and a fine glass ceiling installed over its central courtyard. Interactive exhibitions have been added to the collection of model ships, marine art, globes, maps and booty from far-flung lands – all of which document the long, illustrious history of maritime achievement of the Dutch. Visitors can explore the full-size re-creation of the Dutch East India company ship Amsterdam, docked outside. The ship left for Asia in 1749 but was wrecked off the English coast near Hastings – where it still lies.

SCIENCE CENTER NEMO

Next to the museum, and recognisable by its vast ship-like bulk and huge green outer walls, is the **Science Center NEMO**  (www.nemosciencemuseum.nl; Tue–Sun 10am–5pm, also Mon from May–Aug and during Dutch school holidays). Designed by architect Renzo Piano, the centre was created to bring the latest science and technology into the hands of visitors, whatever their age.

The location of NEMO itself is a technological marvel. It sits high above the entrance to the IJ tunnel, which takes six lanes of traffic under the IJ waterway to Amsterdam's northern suburbs and beyond. Inside there are five floors of activities and hosts of interactive, hands-on experiments for all ages. You can take a DNA journey, fit inside a soap bubble or see how lightning works. NEMO's huge roof terrace provides great views of the city.

The unmissable, ship-shaped NEMO

Café culture at Leidseplein

THE SOUTHWEST

The southwest section takes on a fan shape from the centre of the city, widening as it travels out and encompassing the major art museums.

MUNTPLEIN

Our starting point is **Muntplein**, at the junction of the River Amstel and the Singel canal. Although only a small square, and cut by numerous tramlines, it has a particularly beautiful tower – **Munttoren** ⓴ (Mint Tower), originally a medieval gate guarding the entrance to the city. It was damaged by fire in 1619, and the clock tower was added by Hendrick de Keyser during the renovations. In 1699 the carillon was installed, and this still fills the air with its tinkling sounds. During the war with France in 1672, when Amsterdam's supply of money was cut off, the tower became the city mint, and the name has stuck.

BLOEMENMARKT

In the shadow of the tower and partly floating on the Singel (the medieval protective moat for the city) is the **Bloemenmarkt** ㉑ (Flower Market). The daily market has been held for centuries, when the flower sellers would arrive by canal with boats laden with blooms. Today the stalls (selling clogs and delftware as well as flowers) still float on barges permanently attached to the canal wall. The blooms they sell bring a splash of colour to even the dullest Amsterdam day.

Stroll along the market until you reach Koningsplein and turn left down Leidsestraat. This major shopping street is always busy because it links one of the largest squares in the city to the central area.

LEIDSEPLEIN

At the end of Leidsestraat is **Leidseplein** ㉒, the busiest square in the city, with tourist bars and cafés spilling onto it; it's a major nightlife focus, too. Look out for a small grassy area, with sculptures of life-size iguanas and other large lizards. The narrow streets leading off the square are full of cinemas, concert halls and intimate live venues.

Fresh flowers for sale at Bloemenmarkt

In summer you will find several different street performers vying for your euros. It's a place where talented music students play classical pieces, or musicians from around the world play their traditional tunes, taking their turn with jugglers, mime artists and magicians. Whatever the time of year, as the sun sets, the neon lights are switched on, and people flock to enjoy the restaurants and nightclubs that keep the square buzzing until the early hours of the morning.

On the western side of Leidseplein you will find the **Stadsschouwburg** (Municipal

Theatre; http://stadsschouwburgamsterdam.nl), built in 1894. Across the square is the **American Hotel** (www.hampshire-hotels.com), an Art Nouveau treasure and national monument completed in 1902. Non-residents can visit the Café Américain on the ground floor to enjoy the sumptuous surroundings.

VONDELPARK

Turn left after Leidseplein and across the Singel you will find the **Holland Casino Amsterdam** and the **Lido Club** on your left (www.hollandcasino.nl). On your right, across Stadhouderskade, is a narrow gate into **Vondelpark ㉓**, a park that has been called 'the lungs of Amsterdam'. It was founded in 1865 after a number of philanthropic city fathers decided there was a need for a genteel recreation area for the city's population, many of whom lived in overcrowded slums. The park was named after the Netherlands' premier poet and playwright Joost van den Vondel and designed in the English fashion of the times. It originally served as a private park, paid for by the wealthy families who lived around it. Today its 46 hectares (120 acres) have ponds, farm animals, flocks

A STAR IS BORN

Close to the Museumplein is the new **Modern Contemporary Museum Amsterdam** (MOCO; www.mocomuseum.com; daily 10am–6pm), which features works by the so-called rock stars of contemporary art, including street art legend Banksy and the king of pop art Andy Warhol. Occupying the former Villa Alsberg, this museum was founded by art dealers Kim and Lionel Logchies, and opened its doors in 2016. Planned exhibitions include works by the best 20th-century and contemporary artists including Pablo Picasso, Salvador Dalí, Damien Hirst, Os Gemeos, Brian Donnelly (KAWS) or Maya Hayuk.

of parakeets, jogging tracks and cycle paths.

MUSEUMPLEIN

Only five minutes to the south of Leidseplein is the Museum Quarter, for many visitors the main reason for their visit to Amsterdam. Here, three of the most important art collections in Europe sit side by side, allowing visitors to walk

Vondelpark, 'the lungs of Amsterdam'

from one to the next in a matter of moments. Although all very different in appearance, they are brought together by an open space, which is called, not surprisingly, **Museumplein**.

RIJKSMUSEUM

The highlight of any art lover's trip to Amsterdam is the **Rijksmuseum** ㉔ (State Museum; www.rijksmuseum.nl; daily 9am–5pm, tickets bookable online), which is home to the greatest collection of Dutch art in the world. Following a €375 million, decade-long restoration and extension, the museum reopened its doors in 2013. The transformation is remarkable, both for the building and the presentation of the collection. The elegance of Pierre Cuypers' original Victorian Gothic buildings has been restored, and the galleries have been redesigned so that visitors can follow a chronological journey through the collection. For the first time the decorative and historic exhibits are shown alongside the artistic treasures, giving a real sense of time. The former gloomy entrance has been transformed by a soaring light-filled atrium, with a stylish café, book and souvenir shops. New galleries include the Asian pavilion, surrounded by water, the 20th century galleries, the Special Collections (fascinating objets d'art from the museum's rich holding) and newly opened gardens with sculpture. But the real magnet still remains the Gallery of Honour, hung with Rembrandts, Vermeers and other jewels of the Dutch Golden Age.

Restoration took 10 years instead of the intended five, due largely to the lengthy battle with the powerful Dutch cycling lobby who objected to the proposed closure of the cycle thoroughfare which runs smack through the museum, separating the two courtyards. The cyclists triumphed, their route was retained and the architects came up with an ingenious solution of digging down five metres, using boats and divers, to create the atrium, finally linking the two courtyards.

Cuypers' original building was designed around Rembrandt's *Night Watch*; and this masterpiece still retains pride of place at the head of the Gallery of Honour – the only work among 8,000 exhibits to be returned after restoration to its original location.

The Rijksmuseum after its decade-long facelift

The painting – one of 20 works by the artist in the collection – is properly entitled *The Company of Captain Frans Banning Cocq and Lieutenant Willem van Ruytenburch*. The work, which was commissioned by the company for its barracks, is remarkable for its lack of formality and very different from the accepted style of the day. Its size is impressive, yet it was originally even larger. It had to be trimmed to make it fit into the Town Hall where it was moved in 1715. In 2016, the *Night Watch* was joined by two more Rembrandt masterpieces, when the Netherlands and France jointly bought the wedding portraits of Marten Soolmans and Oopjen Coppitby. Please note that due to their joint Dutch/French ownership, the pieces spend half their time at the Rijksmuseum and the other half at the Louvre.

The Night Watch Gallery at the Rijksmuseum

Johannes Vermeer is well represented, and his effective use of light can be seen in *The Milkmaid*, (c.1658–60) and *Woman Reading a Letter* (c.1663) two of the gallery's best-loved pieces. There are paintings by Frans Hals, the founding artist of the Dutch School, along with a collection of Dutch artists who were influenced or schooled by the masters. Rembrandt was a prolific teacher and his pupils produced work so similar to his that many were mistaken for the great artist's work.

Look out also for the painting by a lesser-known artist, Gerrit Adriaensz Berckheyde, of *Herengracht* in 1672, when its grand houses were being completed. The scene has no trees and shows the 'Gentlemen's Canal' in pristine condition.

VAN GOGH MUSEUM

Visible just behind the Rijksmuseum are the modern lines of the **Van Gogh Museum** ㉕ (www.vangoghmuseum.nl; daily

DUTCH MASTERS OLD AND NEW

The Golden Age of the Netherlands (roughly speaking, the 17th century) produced a number of brilliant artists who left a rich legacy of work. In the years since, there have been further shining lights.

Frans Hals (c.1580–1666) is considered the founder of the Dutch School of realistic painting. He introduced 'the captured moment' to fine art – the glance or casual expression not formerly seen in formal portraits. His celebrated portrait *The Laughing Cavalier* is in the Rijksmuseum.

Rembrandt Harmenszoon van Rijn (1606–69). Today, the best-known artist of the Dutch School, Rembrandt revolutionised painting with his informal composition and use of light. He lived in Amsterdam for much of his life. Some of his best work is in the Rijksmuseum and a collection of his sketches at his house (Museum Het Rembrandthuis).

Johannes (Jan) Vermeer (1632–75) painted only around 30 works, but his attention to detail and sympathetic use of light later made his work famous. His painting of The Milkmaid is in the Rijksmuseum.

Jacob van Ruisdael (c.1628–82). Master of the landscape, he had the ability to create an almost photographic realism. A number of his works are in the Rijksmuseum.

Vincent van Gogh (1853–90) developed his strong use of form and colour after he settled in Provence. Suffering from mental illness, he died after shooting himself just before his revolutionary work was recognised. The Van Gogh Museum has more than 200 of his paintings.

Piet Mondrian (1872–1944) brought painting down to its essence, with stark abstract lines and blocks created using primary colours. Examples of his work can be viewed at the Stedelijk Museum.

9am–5pm, Fri until 10pm),
devoted to the work of the
Dutch master. The main
building, by Gerrit Rietveld,
opened in 1973; a sepa-
rate circular wing, by Kisho
Kurokawa, hosts temporary
exhibitions. The museum's
gallery walls newly painted in
stormy greys, blues and yel-
lows, reflect the canvasses

A self-portrait at the Van Gogh Museum

they display. There are over
200 paintings and 500 draw-
ings by the painter, covering all periods of his troubled career.
Vincent's brother Theo van Gogh, who also kept more than 800
letters written by his brother, collated the bulk of the collection.

Vincent's working life was short but frenetic, interspersed
with periods of manic depression, and his paintings reflect
his moods. His 1885 work *The Potato Eaters* shows the hard
lives endured by the rural poor among whom he lived at
this time. Contrast this with the superb vibrant colours of
The Bedroom in Arles and *Vase with Sunflowers*, both painted
after Vincent moved to Provence in 1888.

STEDELIJK MUSEUM AND SURROUNDING AREA

Next door to the Van Gogh Museum is the city's collection
of modern and contemporary art and design, the **Stedelijk
Museum** ㉖ (Municipal Museum; www.stedelijk.nl; daily
10am–6pm, Fri until 10pm). The museum reopened in 2012
after eight years of renovation and extension. The famous
1895 facade is neoclassical, with figures such as the architect and sculptor Hendrick de Keyser (1565–1621) gazing
down on the passing crowds. It was built specifically to

house the private art collection of Sophia de Bruyn, who then bequeathed it to the city in 1890. A striking white extension has been added to the stately facade, nicknamed The Bathtub, for reasons that will become apparent if you view it from Museumplein. This provides a lobby, shop, restaurant and a large space for temporary exhibitions. The museum's permanent collection includes pieces by Marc Chagall, Picasso, Monet, Cézanne and Matisse. There is also a comprehensive examination of the art and design movement known as De Stijl (The Style), which swept through the Netherlands just after World War I.

DIAMOND TERRITORY

If you feel culturally exhausted after your 'museum-fest', the streets around Museumplein offer some exciting retail therapy. Walk across Paulus Potterstraat from the Van Gogh

Buildings line Herengracht Canal

Museum and you will find **Coster Diamonds** (http://costerdiamonds.com; daily 9am–5pm, free guided tours), one of the oldest 'houses' in the city, where you can watch diamonds being polished and maybe buy a carat or two. For the most upmarket shopping street of the Netherlands,

> **Tip**
>
> It is worth making the short detour to the old Heineken brewery at Stadhouderskade 78. The **Heineken Experience** (www.heineken.com) includes an interactive tour of the old plant and tasting of the famous beer.

head for P.C. Hoofstraat, running parallel to Paulus Potterstraat; or for art and antiques explore the Spiegelkwartier across the bridge from the Rijksmuseum. For culture of a more musical nature go to the world-famous Royal **Concertgebouw** (www.concertgebouw.nl) on Van Baerlstraat, home to the orchestra of the same name. The concert hall celebrated its 125th anniversary in 2013 and was awarded royal status. The acoustics are almost perfect, even though the designer of the building, Adolf Leonard van Gendt, had no experience in this specialised area.

NIEUWE SPIEGELSTRAAT AND THE GOLDEN BEND

If you want to stroll back to town after your visit to the museums, then walk through the open courtyard that cuts through the centre of the Rijksmuseum, across Stadhouderskade and on to narrow Spiegelgracht and its continuation **Nieuwe Spiegelstraat**. This centre of antiques and art galleries has some wonderful windows to gaze into.

Walk north along the length of Nieuwe Spiegelstraat and you will eventually reach Herengracht at its most spectacular point. When it was first dug, and the lots of land sold, it was soon realised that this section of the canal (between Vijzelstraat and Leidsestraat) would have the largest houses inhabited by the richest families in the city. For this reason it has become known as the **Gouden Bocht** (Golden Bend). Many of these grand old buildings now house banks and financial institutions.

THE NORTHWEST

THE BEGIJNHOF

The northwest section abuts the centre, beginning at **Kalver-straat**, the rather brash, shopping street that cuts the centre of Amsterdam from north to south. In a small square called **Spui** you will find a book market on Friday. Off the north side of the square, a narrow alleyway, Gedempte Begijnensloot, leads to the entrance of the **Begijnhof** ㉗ (www.begijnhof amsterdam.nl; daily 9am–5pm; free), a haven of tranquillity in the centre of the city.

Smoking

Smoking is not allowed in public buildings or on public transport, and only in the Rookzone (Smoking Area) on station platforms. Nor is it allowed in hotels, restaurants, cafés and bars, except in separate enclosed areas in which no food or drinks are served, and in small bars operated only by the owner. Smoking coffee shops are permitted to sell up to 5 grams of cannabis to those over-18 but not products containing tobacco.

The cluster of buildings around a garden was set aside in 1346 for the benefit of the Beguines, members of a lay Catholic sisterhood. They lived simple lives and in return for their lodgings undertook to care for the sick and educate the poor. Although nothing remains of the 14th-century houses, No. 34 is **Het Houten Huys**, Amsterdam's oldest house, dating from around 1425.

The Catholic chapel dates from 1671 when it was built in a style designed to disguise

English Reformed Church, Begijnhof

its purpose. The spectacular stained-glass windows depict the Miracle of Amsterdam. In the centre of the courtyard is the English Reformed Church, where the Pilgrim Fathers worshipped before setting off to the New World (they came here from England before leaving for America).

The last Beguine died in 1971 and today, although the houses are still offered only to single women of the Christian faith, the women are not expected to undertake lay work.

AMSTERDAM MUSEUM

Behind the Begijnhof is the old **Sint-Luciënklooster** (Convent of St Lucy), which became the city orphanage after the Alteration, although it was open only to well-to-do orphans; the poor had to fend for themselves. It was extended several times, including a wing designed by Hendrick de Keyser, and opened in 1975 as the **Amsterdam Museum** ㉘ (www.amsterdammuseum.nl; daily 10am–5pm). Its rooms reveal details of the development of this fascinating city through plans, paintings, archaeological finds and a multimedia DNA exhibition that breaks down a thousand years of history into seven periods.

The Golden Age is brought to life in rooms 5–12, but there is also an interesting section on 20th- and 21st-century Amsterdam, covering the Nazi occupation, and efforts to protect and preserve the city. Tiny details, such as a relief above the Kalverstraat entrance, asking people to support the upkeep of the orphanage, point to the building's original purpose.

THE DAM

Once out of the museum, walk north. Take Kalverstraat or, if you find it a little too busy for comfort, take Rokin, which runs parallel to Kalverstraat to the right. This wide street was once a canal, part of which was drained and filled in

The magnificent Koninklijk Paleis

to allow better access for modern forms of transport. On the far side of the canal is the elegant Georgian facade of the **Allard Pierson Museum** (www.allardpierson museum.nl; Tue–Fri 10am–5pm, Sat–Sun 1–5pm), the archaeological collection of the University of Amsterdam, which has superb temporary

Rembrandt's ruins

The medieval **Stadhuis** (Town Hall) burnt down in 1652 while the building that is now Koninklijk Paleis was being built to replace it. Rembrandt provided a record of the scene when, curiously, he drew the old building in ruins, rather than the new one rising beside it.

exhibitions. Another couple of minutes will bring you to the **Dam** ㉙, the symbolic heart of the city.

KONINKLIJK PALEIS

The Dam is a wide cobbled square dominated by the ornate **Koninklijk Paleis** (Royal Palace; www.paleisamsterdam.nl; open most days 10am–5pm; see website for further details), which was completed in 1655. It was originally built as the Town Hall, facing the landing wharfs along Damrak, which at that time would have been busy with ships. The classical design by Jacob van Campen gives some indication of the confidence of the city in the Golden Age – a statue of Atlas carrying the world on his shoulders sits astride the rear of the building, and in the sumptuous interior, only the best materials were used.

When Louis Bonaparte, brother of Napoleon, became king of Holland in 1806, he demanded a palace suitable for his position and in 1808 requisitioned the Town Hall. He furnished it with the finest pieces of the time and left them all behind only two years later when he was forced out of power. It has remained a royal palace ever since, used for ceremonial occasions only. As long as the palace is not in use for ceremonies, you can visit the grand interior with its wealth of reliefs, chandeliers, marble sculptures and paintings by pupils of Rembrandt.

NIEUWE KERK, NATIONAAL MONUMENT AND WAXWORKS

Beside the palace is the **Nieuwe Kerk** (New Church; www.nieuwekerk.nl; daily Mar–Sept 10am–6pm, Oct–Feb 11am–5pm generally, times may vary), built before the palace, but not the oldest church in the city, hence its name. The church has suffered several fires during the course of its history and was stripped of all its treasures during the Alteration. The pulpit is notable for being extremely ornate for a Protestant place of worship. The church is now used as a cultural centre.

Across the Dam is the stark, white **Nationaal Monument** commemorating the role of the Dutch in World War II.

The Nationaal Monument

On the Dam's south side stands **Madame Tussauds** (www.madametussauds.com; daily 10am–10pm; times may vary), with a panorama recreating Amsterdam's Golden Age, as well as wax models of celebrities.

Magna Plaza shopping centre

Make your way behind the Royal Palace to Raadhuisstraat, which leads to the northern canal ring (Herengracht, Keizersgracht and Prinsengracht). Immediately behind the palace is **Magna Plaza**, built in 1899 as the main post office, although its Gothic architecture was considered far too ornate for a civil service department. It is now home to the city's premier shopping mall (www.magnaplaza.nl).

AROUND RAADHUISSTRAAT

Raadhuisstraat is the main thoroughfare to the northwestern canal ring and is busy with trams and buses. It will take you quickly to the main attractions of the area but it is not the prettiest or quietest route. Wandering the smaller alleys and lanes to the north and south is much more fulfilling.

Just off Raadhuisstraat, Herengracht 168, is a superb 17th-century residence. The grey sandstone house was built in neoclassical style by architect Philips Vingboons and sports the city's first neck gable. The red-brick **Huis Bartolotti** at Nos 170–2 is an ornate Dutch Renaissance mansion built in 1617 by Hendrick de Keyser and his son Pieter, with illuminated 18th-century ceilings by Jacob de Wit.

WESTERKERK

Follow Raadhuisstraat until you reach the **Westerkerk** ⓿ (www.westerkerk.nl; Mon–Fri Mon–Sat 10am–3pm, Apr–Oct also Sat 11am–3pm), set in its own square on the left and overlooking Prinsengracht. Hendrick de Keyser designed this church, one of his last commissions, in 1619. It is reputed to be the burial place of Rembrandt, but no one knows the exact location of the grave (which may no longer exist). One of his pupils, Gerard de Lairesse, painted the organ panels, added in 1686. In summer you can climb the Westerkerk's tower, the tallest in the city at 83m (273ft), offering incomparable views. The crown on top is a replica of one presented to the city in 1489 by Maximilian I, Holy Roman Emperor.

ANNE FRANK HOUSE

Turn left beyond the church to Prinsengracht 263, just an ordinary canal house-cum-office but made famous world-wide by events here in World War II. During the Nazi occupation a young girl, her family and a small group of others hid for two years here in an attempt to avoid deportation. It is, of course, **Anne Frank Huis** ⓷ (Anne Frank House; www.annefrank.org; daily Apr–Oct 9am–10pm,– Mar 9am–7pm Sat until 9pm; closed Yom Kippur).

Wooden bookcase at the Anne Frank Huis

Anne wrote a diary that paints a clear and terrifying picture of the life the family lived. It comes to an eerie stop only a few days

Looking down from the Westerkerk tower

before the family was betrayed and sent to concentration camps. Of the eight people in hiding, only Anne's father survived – Anne died of typhus only weeks before the war ended – and after the war, in 1947, he published the diary, which became a symbol for the oppression of humankind.

The house, built in 1635, has been left much as it was at the time Anne hid here. It opened as a museum in 1960. The secret rooms upstairs, where the family spent the daylight hours, are stark and bleak. A couple of magazine pin-ups still adorn one wall. The wooden bookcase, which hid the doorway to their refuge, is still in situ, propped open for visitors to climb the few stairs. Downstairs were the offices and warehouses of Mr Frank's business, which were recreated in a multimillion-dollar development. Two adjacent buildings have been acquired and refurbished, adding exhibition and audiovisual space, without compromising No. 263 itself. You can see videos of Anne's story and of Amsterdam under occupation, along with photos and artefacts.

The Anne Frank Huis also acts as an education centre and resource for political and philosophical groups fighting oppression in the present day.

THE JORDAAN

Cross Prinsengracht to reach the area of the city known as the **Jordaan** ㉜. Built as housing for workers and artisans in the early 17th century, it extends roughly from the far bank of Prinsengracht to Lijnbaansgracht and from Brouwersgracht (Brewers Canal) south to Leidseplein. Many of the streets were named after fragrant flowers but this was not the prettiest or sweetest smelling area of Amsterdam in its heyday.

Overcrowding was rife and with industries such as fabric-dyeing carried out on the ground floors, it was an unsanitary place to live.

The rowing lake in Amsterdamse Bos

Its name is said to derive from the French word *jardin*, since a large contingent of French Huguenots came to live here to escape political persecution. Today, the Jordaan has been revived and become a fashionable residential location. You'll find many bars, restaurants,

Saving the Jordaan

In the 1970s, parts of the Jordaan were earmarked for demolition, but thanks to widespread protests, the narrow streets were preserved, complete with period features such as these antique street lamps.

galleries and boutiques in the area. It's a good place to browse for an unusual souvenir.

Rozengracht, a hectic street, marks a Jordaan dividing line. The section to the north of here, and more particularly above Westerstraat, is a maze of alleys, quiet restaurants and thriving workshops, and retains many of its working-class roots. It has many true Jordaaners – traditionally, those who live close enough to the Westertoren to be able to hear the tinkling of its bells – independent-minded students, crafts- and tradespeople born and bred in the quarter. The section below Rozengracht is more gentrified, with individualistic shops on lovely side streets adjacent to the larger canals, and numerous brown cafés.

AMSTERDAMSE BOS

The Netherlands suffered economic stagnation during the late 1920s and 1930s, as did the majority of other developed countries. One of the methods used to relieve the problems of unemployment was to organise large government-funded community projects, such as the **Amsterdamse Bos** ❸ (Amsterdam Wood; www.amsterdamsebos.nl), which created the largest recreation area in the city. The park is on the southern fringes of the city and can be reached by

A houseboat on Bloemgracht canal

bus 170,172 or 174 from Centraal Station. On Sundays, you can also travel to the park on the historic **Museum Tram** (www.museumtramlijn.org) which departs from Haarlemmermeer station.

In 1967, it was enlarged to its present 800 hectares (2,000 acres). The trees and plants are now well established, and the wood has become an important habitat for birds, small mammals and insects, making this an ecological centre as well as a park. It has meadows, woodland and a huge lake for rowing, sailing and hourly rowing-boat hire. It features nature reserves, animal enclosures and a botanical garden. With around 48km (30 miles) of bicycle paths and close to 160km (100 miles) of footpaths, there is room for everybody. The stables at Amsterdamse Bos offer woodland horse rides, a perfect way to clear the city air from your system (Amsterdamse Manege; http://eng.de amsterdamsemanege.nl). There is also an open-air theatre, which holds performances in the summer.

EXCURSIONS

There are plenty of places within easy day-trip range of Amsterdam, a selection of which we cover in this chapter. Heading out of the city for a day (or two) will enable you to discover the Netherlands on a different level, whether climbing inside a windmill, walking along an historic canal that inspired the young Rembrandt, or eating pancakes in a pastoral village.

Some of the excursions covered below are served by coach tours (ask for details at the tourist office, see page 128), although you can also find your own way by bus, train, bicycle or rented car.

VILLAGES TO THE NORTH

To the north of Amsterdam are several small towns that not only provide a contrast to the city landscape, they also take you to the heart of agricultural North Holland.

CLOGS

Clogs, the native footwear of the Netherlands, are still worn by some Dutch in rural areas and they find them as practical as they ever were. Clogs are traditionally made from poplar or willow – two trees that are commonly planted on the river and *polder* banks because they can soak up as much as 1,000 litres (265 gallons) of water per tree per day, keeping water levels under control. The shoes are carved from freshly felled wood and after being shaped are left to dry and harden.

Clogs are traditionally worn two sizes larger than a person's shoe size, with thick socks to fit loosely to avoid rubbing the skin. Only ceremonial clogs (and those for tourists) are painted; everyday pairs are simple and unadorned. You often see farmers and sailors wearing them. Some road workers and deliverymen also find them more comfortable than standard protective boots.

ZAANSE SCHANS

One such village is **Zaanse Schans** ❸❹ (www.zaanseschans.nl), a patch of archetypal Dutch landscape just a few kilometres north of Amsterdam centre, near the town of Zaandam. This is a living museum created in 1960, which has brought together a number of farmhouses, windmills, dairies and barns – agricultural buildings that would have been demolished had they not been relocated here. Zaanse Schans has working mills, craft shops, cheese-making factories and a clog workshop on a canalside. You are free to explore at your own pace and maybe enjoy a *pannenkoek* (pancake) while you're there.

BROEK IN WATERLAND AND MONNICKENDAM

Broek in Waterland is a village situated just north of the city environs. A small collection of quaint wooden houses, it is surrounded by canals and streams.

Traditional windmills at Zaanse Schans

Further north is **Monnick-endam** ㉟, once a large fishing port on the Zuiderzee which lost its *raison d'être* when the Afsluitdijk was completed in 1932, creating the freshwater lake called the IJsselmeer. The pretty, gabled buildings that line the main street were once cottages for fisherfolk, and the small port still has a

Windmills

After the invention of the first sawmill in 1592, more than 1,000 windmills were built in the Zaan region, many to provide power for sawing timber for the Zaan shipyards. Eight mills can be seen at Zaanse Schans today, and a ninth is being rebuilt.

fleet of ships. Many are now in private hands, or serve as pleasure boats in the summer season. There is also a large, private marina filled with sailing boats that head out onto the open water on any sunny weekend. Walk around the old port to find vestiges of the traditional lifestyle. A few families still fish for eels and process them in small 'factories' along the quayside. In summer you can buy them from stalls in the town. There are also some good fish restaurants around the harbour.

MARKEN

Just 5km (3 miles) beyond Monnickendam is **Marken** ㊱, one of the most beautiful villages in the Netherlands and home to a community of Calvinist Dutch whose traditions reach back hundreds of years. Situated on an island, Marken had no vehicle access until 1957, when a causeway was opened, linking the village to the mainland. Today the community welcomes visitors but not their cars, which must be left in a large car park on the outskirts.

A few of the older inhabitants of this close-knit community still wear traditional Dutch costume. You can walk through the village with its pretty painted wooden houses to the picture-perfect harbour. Between Monnickendam and

Marken, the causeway leads into open water that is home to thousands of birds in summer. The native herons, ducks and moorhens see many species of migratory birds that fly north for the summer and return south as winter approaches. Head out on the smooth flat road towards the old lighthouse on a lonely promontory at the far end of Marken island.

VOLENDAM AND EDAM

North of Marken and Monnickendam is **Volendam**, a Catholic counterpart to Protestant Marken. It is the village most changed by tourism, with cafés and souvenir shops lining the harbour. Volendam is still noted for its fish (there are several good restaurants and herring stands) and for distinctive local dress, especially the women's winged lace caps.

The town of **Edam** ③⑦, famed for its red- or yellow-rinded cheese, has a pretty **Kaaswaag** (Cheese Weigh House; www.

Traditional boats moored in Monnickendam

edamcheeseshop.com) dating from 1592. Look out for the **Kwakelbrug**, wide enough only for single-file pedestrian traffic. The centre of town has an unusual paved overlock, the **Damsluis**, just below the **Captain's House** (1540). Despite its world renown, Edam is still unspoiled and there are some pretty restaurants where you can enjoy lunch before heading back to the city.

The road to Marken's old lighthouse

HAARLEM

Haarlem ㊳, just 19km (12 miles) west of Amsterdam, was the home of Antwerp-born Frans Hals, father of the Dutch School of painting. The centre of town is a maze of narrow streets full of historic buildings, which fall under the shadow of the 15th-century **Sint-Bavokerk** (St Bavo's Church; www.rkbavo.nl; Mon–Fri 10am–4pm, summer also Sat 11am–2.30pm), an enormous Gothic edifice – also known as the **Grote Kerk** (Great Church) – which contains one of the finest organs in Europe. Handel and Mozart both played the instrument, and you can hear it on summer Saturdays at 3pm, when free recitals fill the church with music. Across Lepelstraat from the church is the 1603 **Vleeshal** (meat market).

On Groot Heiligland to the south, the **Frans Hals Museum** (www.franshalsmuseum.nl; Tue–Sat 11am–5pm, Sun noon–5pm) is a suitable testimony to the town's most famous son, who was still painting in his eighties. The museum was opened in 1913 at the site of a home for old men.

On the banks of the River Spaarne is the **Teylers Museum** (www.teylersmuseum.eu; Tue–Fri 10am–5pm, Sat–Sun 11am–5pm), founded by silk merchant Pieter Teyler van der Hulst in 1778 and said to be the Netherlands' oldest public collection. Teyler, having no heir, bequeathed his fortune to the advancement of the arts and sciences, and there is an interesting collection of scientific instruments, fossils, minerals and paintings and drawings by old masters including Rembrandt.

FLORAL GLORY

Every spring, from early April to the end of May, the fields south of Haarlem and Amsterdam erupt in a rainbow of colour, which stretches as far as the eye can see. Dutch tulips attract thousands of visitors for these few weeks of beauty.

Another attraction for flower lovers is **Keukenhof** ❸❾ (www.keukenhof.nl; late Mar–late May daily 8am–7.30pm), a 28-hectare (69-acre) showpiece garden near the town of Lisse, that welcomes the public. You'll find a host of spectacular crocus, hyacinth and narcissus blooms along with the tulips. The gardens are planted with stately beech and oak trees, enhanced by pretty windmills that add to the authentic Dutch feel. There is also a restaurant and gift shop where you can buy bulbs, blooms and souvenirs.

Flowers in Keukenhof

In **Aalsmeer** ❹⓿ you can visit the vast **Flora Holland** (Flower Auction; www.floraholland.com; Mon–Wed and Fri 7am–11am, Thu 7am–9am) at Legmeerdijk. The earlier you arrive the better. Millions of blooms are auctioned then dispatched around the world within hours. It's fascinating to watch the action, as miniature trains carry the flowers through the auction hall for the buyers to assess, and a large electronic bid-taker on the wall reflects the current bidding price. The sheer size of the auction house is what gives pause for thought – the walkway for spectators is 1.6km (1 mile) long and workers cross the area by bike.

LEIDEN

The rich history and university atmosphere makes Leiden  an interesting

Riverside Teylers Museum

place to visit. Just a half-hour by train from Amsterdam, this medieval city, famous for cloth-making and brewing industries, joined the Dutch Revolt against Spain and was besieged. It eventually rallied after the dykes were broken and the land was flooded, enabling a rescue fleet to sail directly across the countryside and save the city.

Rembrandt was born in Leiden, as were other Dutch Masters such as Gerrit Dou, Jan Steen, Gabriel Metsu and Jan van Gooyen. This is also where the Pilgrim Fathers formed a community in 1608, seeking refuge from religious persecution in England. Leiden University is the oldest and probably the most prestigious in the Netherlands, with alumni including René Descartes and the 17th-century lawyer, Hugo Grotius.

Visit the **Molen Museum De Valk** (De Valk Windmill Museum; https://molenmuseumdevalk.nl; Tue–Sat 10am–5pm, Sun 1–5pm) on Tweede Binnenvestgracht, and the **Museum De Lakenhal Leiden** (www.lakenhal.nl/en; closed till 2018) on Oude Singel, with rooms illuminating Leiden's history. Two concentric canals ring the inner city, so a stretch of water is never far away, and there are many bridges to cross. Make your way to the marketplace where the old and new branches of the Rhine meet and open markets are held on Wednesday and Saturday. Then cross the bridge to Oude Rijn and turn right towards the **Burcht**, Leiden's 12th-century castle. Have a drink or a meal at the Koetshuis brasserie-restaurant in the courtyard (www.koetshuisdeburcht.nl). The **Hortus Botanicus** (Leiden Botanical Garden; www.hortusleiden.nl; Apr–Oct daily 10am–6pm, Nov–Mar Tue–Sun 10am–4pm) at Rapenburg 73 are also worth a visit.

ALKMAAR

Dutch cheeses are world renowned, and the small red and yellow Edam and Gouda rounds can be found in supermarkets and grocery stores in just about every country of the Western world. However, in the Netherlands, cheese isn't so much an industry as a way of life, and tradition still has a part to play in the production and distribution of the product.

Alkmaar ㊷ is a small town 30km (19 miles) north of Amsterdam. It has been the centre of cheese production for many centuries and

Make Love Not War

Alkmaar's municipal museum, Stedelijk Museum Alkmaar (https://stedelijkmuseumalkmaar.nl; Tue–Sun 11am–5pm, Fri also 5–7pm) on Canadaplein, is housed in a Renaissance guild house. It contains the 16th-century *Siege of Alkmaar*; bizarrely, the painting shows a couple making love while the battle rages.

Alkmaar cheese porters

is now the only town that still has a cheese market, held every Friday morning (www.kaasmarkt.nl/en; 10am–2pm) from early April until early September. There is also another busy market in town on Friday, selling goods and produce other than cheese.

The 14th-century **Waaggebouw** was a chapel before being converted into a weigh house. On Friday the square in front of it becomes a showcase of cheese, when rounds of cheese are piled there waiting to be weighed. Porters, dressed in white trousers, white shirts and coloured hats, transport them on wooden sleds with shoulder harnesses and playfully attempt to be the fastest, much to the amusement of the crowds.

Nearby, the **Grote Kerk** (Great Church; www.grotekerk-alk maar.nl; June–Sept Tue–Sun 11am–5pm, Apr–May Thu–Sat 11am–5pm; free) contains the tomb of the count of Holland, Floris V, who granted Amsterdam its rights to carry goods toll-free in the 13th century. In a sense he started the economic life of the city and could be said to be its founding father.

WHAT TO DO

SHOPPING

Amsterdam is a gold mine for those who like to browse. The narrow streets of the centre, the canal rings and the Jordaan area are home to myriad small, independent boutiques, where you can wander for hours in search of an individual gift.

Most museums have good gift shops, especially the Rijksmuseum, the Van Gogh Museum on Museumplein, the Stedelijk Museum, Jewish Historical Museum, Maritime Museum and Science Center NEMO. The Rijksmuseum and Van Gogh Museum have an additional shared shop on Museumplein.

Amsterdammers love to shop for their homes. Although many live in small apartments, what they lack in floor space they make up for in the quality of their environments, and interior design stores feature in every shopping area.

MARKETS

Amsterdam has a good number of authentic street markets. Perhaps the most famous market is the partly floating **Bloemenmarkt** (Flower Market), which is held on the Singel every day (8.30am–7pm). As well as beautiful blooms you can buy bulbs and tubers to take home.

In the De Pijp neighbourhood, the lively and colourful Albert Cuyp market (on the eponymous street; http://albert cuyp-markt.amsterdam; Mon to Sat 9.30am–5.30pm) has 260 stalls selling everything from textiles and household goods to fruit, vegetables and freshly-baked waffles. It claims to be Europe's largest daily market. The Pure Markt (www.pure markt.nl) is a large, laid-back affair held every Sunday in a different Amsterdam park. A host of stalls sell food and drink for all tastes, with emphasis on organic or local.

Tulips galore at the Bloemenmarkt

The Noordermarkt (www.noordermarkt-amsterdam.nl), held every Saturday by the Noorderkerk (Northern Church) in the Jordaan, is a farmers' market, renowned for organic products. On Monday mornings the square is the setting for a flea market, with vintage clothing, antiques and curiosities. The Sunday Market (www.sundaymarket.nl) in Cultuurpark Westerpark on the first Sunday of the month, is a fashion, art and design market, held partially in the beautifully renovated buildings of the Westergasfabriek, a former coal gas factory. Every third Sunday of the month (except Sept and Oct) another design market is held at the Museumplein. The Museum Market (www.museum market.nl) also offers great food and atmosphere.

The **flea market** on Waterlooplein, from Monday to Saturday (http://waterlooplein.amsterdam; 9.30am–6pm, is smaller than it used to be, although second hand clothes still feature heavily, along with ethnic wear. The Oost's multicultural Dappermarkt in the east is a flea market particularly popular with locals.

A summer **Antiekmarkt** (Antiques Market) meets at Nieuwmarkt on Sunday from May to October. On Elandsgracht and Looiersgracht in the Jordaan is a market for cheaper antiques, collectables and bric-a-brac. The stalls are found inside a number of old houses, which makes it the perfect place to shop on a rainy day. There is a **Boekenmarkt** (Book Market;

THE NINE STREETS

The Negen Straatjes (Nine Streets) are small alleys that form the ribs linking the Herengracht, Keizersgracht and Prinsengracht canals. The neighbourhood is a shopper's delight with its specialist boutiques, vintage stores, art galleries, antiques and designer clothing outlets. It's also a great place for small restaurants and bars.

www.deboekenmarktophet spui.nl) every Friday on Spui in front of the private entrance to the Begijnhof. Publications in various languages are on sale.

Second-hand clothes at the flea market

WHAT TO BUY

Antiques. The rich legacy of the Dutch colonial period makes Amsterdam an interesting city for antiques. European period furniture mixes with Southeast Asian artefacts and art – there are dealers in almost every specialist area. This is not a place for amateur collectors. Prices are high but so is quality, the expertise of the dealers, and the advice they give. The finest antiques and works of art are found in the Spiegelkwartier district near the Rijksmuseum.

Art. Dozens of small galleries offer everything from classical to pop art. Exhibitions at the major galleries also promote the work of up-and-coming younger artists, as well as established names. Street art is also very much in evidence, especially in the summer. For a more classic form of art, paintings and prints of windmills or canal houses can be found all across the city.

Diamonds. Before World War II, Amsterdam was a major centre for the buying and polishing of diamonds. The industry deteriorated because of the loss of many Jewish families who ran the major diamond houses, but a slow recovery ensured its survival. Today the industry is known for the quality of its polishing and the expertise of its independent traders.

Two main diamond houses in the city are responsible for buying and polishing the majority of the stones. They sell to smaller dealers but also to the public. You will be able to see diamond polishers at work on free guided tours before you buy. The two houses are Gassan (www.gassan.com) at Nieuwe Uilenburgerstraat 173–5, with a branch at Rokin 1–5, at the Dam and **Coster Diamonds** on Paulus Potterstraat 2–6, at Museumplein (www.costerdiamonds.com).

Plants. The Netherlands is famed worldwide for its flowers, and particularly the beautiful spring tulip displays in the fields to the west and southwest of Amsterdam. Yet blooms are produced all year in hothouses scattered across the countryside and can be purchased, along with bulbs, at the Bloemenmarkt on the Singel.

Cigars. There is a small but high-quality cigar industry in the Netherlands offering a wide choice in terms of size and price. **P.G.C. Hajenius**, Rokin 92–6 (www.hajenius.com), have been producing their own brand and importing the best in the world for 170 years. They also have a smoking café if you want to sit and enjoy your cigar on the premises. Their shop, specially built for the company in 1915, has a beautiful Art Deco interior.

Coster Diamonds

Fashion. For designer fashions, visit exclusive P.C. Hooftstraat and neighbouring Van Baerlestraat, which border Museumplein. High street fashion and mainstream department stores are found along Kalverstraat, Leidsestraat and Rokin. Local fashionistas tend to prefer the independent

De Bijenkorf shopping centre

shops, such as those in the **Nine Streets** (see page 84) or along the Utrechtsebuurt. Outlets here include boutiques, some of them quite quirky, designer furniture and homeware, along with some of the city's finest food shops and plenty of tempting little restaurants and cafés. The **Bijenkorf** (https://m.debijenkorf.nl) is Amsterdam's largest and most famous department store, often referred to as the Harrods of Amsterdam. Come for fashions, accessories, homeware, media and travel.

Jenever. Only the Dutch and Belgians produce this alcoholic drink, a kind of hybrid of English gin and German *schnapps*. It is often bottled in distinctive stone flagons, which make wonderful souvenirs– and excellent rustic candlesticks when empty.

Delftware. The pottery style known as Delft (after the city southwest of Amsterdam) was produced across the country during the Golden Age and, in the 1600s, many fine pieces came out of a pottery on Prinsengracht. The blue and white finish is

Blue and white Delftware

standard Delft, and you will find it at many high-class outlets, with prices to match the quality. For an eclectic selection of old and new Delftware, visit **Galleria d'Arte Rinascimento**, Prinsengracht 170 (www.delft-art-gallery.com; tel: 020-622 7509). At **Jorrit Heinen** (www.heinen-delftware.nl), with branches at Prinsengracht 440 (tel: 020-627 8299) and Muntplein 12 (tel: 020-623 2271), you can buy examples of the traditional pottery styles, and some fine modern pieces too.

Other Dutch souvenirs. Wooden clogs feature prominently, either plain or painted in bright colours. Windmills are found everywhere, on tea-towels, T-shirts and fridge magnets and Dutch bulbs are available at all times of the year. If you want something edible then the best bets are *stroopwafels* – the caramel waffle biscuits – or Dutch cheese, such as a small whole Gouda or vacuum-packed farmer's cheese. De Kaaskamer (www.kaaskamer.nl) at Runsstraat 7 has a selection of around 80 cheeses.

ENTERTAINMENT

Over 40 different performances take place every evening of the year in Amsterdam, details of which can be found on the excellent tourist office website: www.iamsterdam.com. Concert halls and theatres are found all across the city with ballet, opera, rock, jazz and classical performances all featured regularly. There are also plenty of venues staging more risqué or avant-garde performances.

The main venues for orchestral and chamber concerts are the **Concertgebouw** (tel: 0900 671 8345; www.concert gebouw.nl) near to Museumplein, home to the renowned Royal Concertgebouw Orchestra; and the **Dutch National Opera & Ballet** (tel: 020-625 5455; www.operaballet.nl) on the banks of the Amstel. The city's newest large musical venue is the **Muziekgebouw aan 't IJ** (tel: 020-788 2000; www.muziekgebouw.nl), on the south bank of the IJ water-way, just east of Centraal Station. It stages performances of modern, world and experimental music. In an annexe is the renowned **Bimhuis** (tel: 020-788 2188; www.bimhuis.nl) jazz and blues club.

The revamped **Koninklijk Theater Carré** (tel: 0900-252 5255; http://web.carre.nl), near the Magere Brug on the Amstel, hosts musicals. **Boom Chicago** (tel: 020-217 0400; www.boomchicago.nl) in Leidseplein is the venue for stand-up comedy in English.

Amsterdam's Concertgebouw

You can book tickets for performances on arrival but popular acts sell out quickly, so reserve in advance if there is something you par-ticularly wish to see. The **Last Minute Ticket Shop** (LMTS) offers a selection of performances at 50 percent discount from 10am daily or from 8am online (www.

lastminuteticketshop.nl). At any given time there will be temporary art exhibitions at galleries and museums around the city. The **EYE Film Institute** (tel: 020-589 1400; www.eyefilm. nl) in Amsterdam–Noord (see page 12) holds regular film showings and during the day films can be watched free of charge from specially-designed pods in the basement.

The **Holland Festival** is a programme of art events in June. In Amsterdam, parks and squares are filled with organised activities, and many galleries and concert halls hold events (tel: 020-523 7787: www.hollandfestival.nl).

Cruising the canals is an excellent way of viewing the city. Many bridges and historic buildings are lit at night, and it is possible to have dinner while cruising along. Most of the canal boat tour companies (see page 122) offer at least one evening cruise that includes wine and cheese or a full dinner.

Paradiso, a popular venue for live music and cultural events

BARS AND CLUBS

Amsterdam bars can be divided into two broad types: the old-fashioned traditional *bruine kroegen* (brown cafés), and contemporary bars and lounges. A small third category, the *proeflokaal* (tasting house), follows the brown-café style. An evergreen brown café is **Hoppe**, Spui 18–20 (tel: 020-420 4420; http://cafehoppe.com), where imbibers spill out onto the pavement in warm weather. In the Jordaan, **'t Smalle**, Egelantiersgracht 12 (tel: 020-623 9617; www.t-smalle.nl), is a popular brown café and tasting house. Head to the redeveloped KNSM Island in the eastern harbour for a much newer café with a traditional patina: **Kanis en Meiland**, Levantkade 127 (tel: 020-737 0674; www.kanisenmeiland.nl). A cool modern spot is **XtraCold Ice Bar**, Amstel 194–6 (tel: 020-320 5700; www.xtracold.com). For cocktails and disco with a panoramic view head up to the **SkyLounge** on the 11th floor of the Double Tree by Hilton Hotel near Centraal Sation (tel: 020 5300 875, www.skyloungeamsterdam.com).

There is no shortage of dance clubs and other nightspots, particularly around Leidseplein and Rembrandtplein, but also scattered around the city. The large multipurpose **Melkweg** (Milky Way; tel: 020-531 8181; www.melkweg.nl) on Lijnbaansgracht is an offbeat arts centre-cum-club, with live music, dance club, disco, experimental plays (some in English) and art exhibitions. On the other side of Leidseplein **Paradiso** (tel: 020-626 4521; www.paradiso.nl) is a converted church with a huge hall where many big names in rock and pop have performed.

On the far side of Vondelpark, the smaller **OCCII**, Amstelveenseweg 134 (tel: 020-671 7778; www.occii.org), is similar, only in a grungier, more cutting-edge vein. A popular central dive is the **Winston**, Warmoesstraat 129 (tel: 020-623 1380;

www.winston.nl), a nightclub and live music venue on the edge of the Red Light District.

SPORTS

FOOTBALL

Football is an incredibly popular sport in the Netherlands, and Ajax (www.ajax.nl), the Amsterdam team, has been one of the most successful in Europe for decades. Ajax play at the Amsterdam ArenA (www.amsterdamarena.nl), a fine modern stadium used for numerous events. It is almost impossible to get tickets in Amsterdam, but you can buy tickets online, or try a travel package on the Ajax website that includes match tickets.

WATERSPORTS

With so much water around, it's not surprising that water-based sports are so popular. Even on city-centre canals you will find pedaloes to hire, operated by Canal Bike (tel: 020-217 0500; www.canal.nl). You can also captain your own boat: Canal Motorboats (www.canalmotorboats.com) has a dock at the Zandhoek marina on Realen Island, west of Centraal Station (tel: 020-422 7007). On the wider waterways you will find rowing and sailing clubs that operate in good weather all year round. Out on the freshwater IJsselmeer lake on any sunny weekend you may see hundreds of white and brown sails. Boats can be hired from Monnickendam and other harbour towns.

CYCLING

Fifty eight percent of Amsterdammers cycle daily and there are more bikes in Amsterdam than permanent residents. Cycling for fun, as well as for commuting, is a major activity. Cycle routes run parallel to most roadways, making longer journeys relatively easy, and sporting groups or families head out to villages such as Monnickendam or Marken. Closer to the centre, a ride through Vondelpark gives you a feeling of being out of the city. If you would like to tour with a group, contact Yellow Bike, Nieuwezijdskolk 29 (tel: 020-620 6940; www.yellowbike.nl). They organise daily tours with English guides from April to October (for bike hire, see page 114).

SKATING

Winter sports have traditionally played a big part in the lives of Amsterdammers. When the rivers and canals freeze, everyone is out on the ice – with long-distance skating through the countryside from town to town on cold, bright Sundays.

Amsterdam ArenA is home to the world-famous Ajax football team

Playing at the TunFun children's activity centre

CHILDREN

Amsterdam has numerous attractions and activities to keep younger visitors occupied. The following is just a small selection.

The hands-on science and technology exhibits and virtual reality games will keep children of all ages entertained at **NEMO** (see page 51). The renovated **Het Scheepvaartmuseum** (Maritime Museum) has special exhibits for children, as well as the huge Dutch East India Company ship to explore (see page 50). The enduringly popular **Madame Tussauds** waxworks (see page 67) presents all the latest stars of music and films. At the **Artis** (see page 48) complex you can explore the zoo, aquarium and planetarium. If looking at the solar system doesn't excite your child then getting close to tigers and elephants might. **Tropenmuseum Junior** (see page 48) introduces children to new cultures in a playful way. Smaller children will enjoy the **TunFun** (www.tunfun.nl) activity centre, beneath the busy traffic junction at Mr Visserplein.

Children usually love **tram rides**; and be sure to take them on a **canal cruise** – seeing a city from a different perspective is great fun and a good education.

Throughout the summer there are activities in major parks and squares. Street theatre, face-painting and hands-on art shows will ignite the kids' enthusiasm. In November, children will enjoy the visit of *Sinterklaas* (St Nicholas), who parades through the streets on horseback, before delivering gifts.

CALENDAR OF EVENTS

25 February Commemoration of the 'February Strike' led by the dockers against the Nazis in 1941, held on Jonas Daniël Meijerplein.

15 March (closest Sunday) Stille Omgang – a silent procession through the city to commemorate the 14th-century 'Miracle' of the Host.

Late March Opening of Keukenhof Gardens, at Lisse 30km (19 miles) southwest of Amsterdam.

27 April (26 April if it falls on a Sunday) Koninginnedag (King's Day), the king's official birthday. Street markets, street parties, fireworks and festivities throughout the city.

4 May Dodenherdenking: National Remembrance Day.

5 May Bevrijdingsdag (Liberation Day): a smaller version of King's Day (see above), held mostly in Vondelpark.

Mid-May Rolling Kitchens. A food truck festival that takes place at Westergasfabriek, an old gas production facility area in Western Amsterdam.

June Holland Festival at the Stadsschouwburg and other venues, featuring theatrical, operatic, dance and musical events. Art Amsterdam (first week of June) presents the best in contemporary Dutch art.

July–September Free concerts and theatre afternoons and evenings in the open-air pavilion in Vondelpark.

Early August Gay Pride: exuberant festival culminating in a colourful boat parade on Prinsengracht.

August Grachtenfestival: a 10 day mid-month feast of classical music, with concerts held at venues along the canals.

Last weekend in August Uitmarkt, a week of free music, dance and theatre previews at major squares around the city.

Mid-November Sinterklaas arrives from Spain and travels through the streets of Amsterdam delivering gifts to the children.

5 December Sinterklaas's saint's day and *Pakjesavon* or Parcels Evening, when Dutch children receive Christmas presents.

31 December New Year's Eve fireworks around Amsterdam harbour and the Nieuwmarkt/Chinatown area.

EATING OUT

Dutch national cuisine includes a limited range of dishes, yet eating out in Amsterdam can be one of the highlights of the trip. The reason? Many of the more than 100 nationalities that inhabit the city have brought their own unique culinary delights to Amsterdam's restaurants. You could stay in the city for over a month and not eat the same style of food twice.

Amsterdam is a café society, and restaurants and bars form a lively part of the social scene.

DUTCH DISHES

Traditional Dutch food is seasonal and based on whatever was harvested from the land or the sea, with light summer dishes

BROWN CAFÉS

Amsterdam's traditional brown cafés (so-called because walls and ceilings have turned brown from age and smoke) are identified by dark, cosy, wooden interiors. The only audible sound is the buzz of lively conversation and the tinkle of glasses being rinsed. Coffee is generally brewed, not machine-made, and if you fancy a snack to go with your beer or spirit, there is usually a plate of olives or cheese. These cafés define the Dutch word *gezelligheid*, which means a state of cosiness or conviviality. This is where local people come for a few beers after work, to play cards, engage in political debates and tell tall tales.

The more elegant and stylish grand cafés in the city serve lunch and desserts, and tend to have high ceilings, more light, reading tables and a wider variety of music than brown cafés. There are also cafés where you can play chess, throw darts, or play pool or billiards. There are men's cafés, women's cafés and even night cafés, which close around 5am.

and hearty, filling winter
foods. Arable farms abound
in the countryside, and meat
dishes do not generally play
a major part in Dutch cuisine. Fish and dairy produce
are always considerably
more prevalent.

The Dutch breakfast *(ont-
bijt)* is a hearty one. Slices of
ham and cheese, and per-
haps boiled eggs with various breads and jam or honey
are accompanied by strong
milky coffee.

Erwtensoep, a hearty Dutch soup

Although Amsterdammers are moving towards lighter,
healthier fare, they still enjoy lunch-time *pannenkoeken*,
pancakes thicker than the French *crêpe* and made fresh
as you order them. You can have savoury ones (made with
eggs and bacon, for instance) or sweet toppings, with
fruit, chocolate and cream, or perhaps even one of each.
Uitsmijter is another interesting and popular lunch dish,
served in Dutch homes and in cafés. It consists of a slice of
bread toasted on one side, on to which a slice of ham and
a fried egg are added.

Broodjes or sandwiches are available with a vast range of
fillings. The local ham and Dutch cheeses are probably the
most authentic if you want to eat local, and the combination
is delicious eaten hot in a *toastje* or toasted sandwich.

Friet (chips, French fries) are served and eaten at any time
of day – you will see the vendors' stalls in squares or on street
corners. They are thickly cut and served with a spoonful of
thick mayonnaise.

Winter dishes are warming and hearty. Start with a bowl of *erwtensoep*, a thick pea soup with chunks of sausage. Served with heavy bread or pumpernickel, it constitutes a meal in itself. The other main type of soup is *bruine bonen soep* made with red kidney beans. This may then be followed by *stamppot*, a purée of potatoes and vegetables (usually kale or cabbage) served with slices of *rookworst* (thick smoked sausage), or *hutspot*, made with beef.

FISH

Fish *(vis)* has been a mainstay of the Dutch diet for many generations. Try halibut *(heilbot)*, cod *(kabeljauw)* or haddock *(schelvis)*, all of which come from the North Sea off the Dutch coast. Local oysters *(oesters)* and mussels *(mosselen)* are especially good, and smoked eel *(gerookte paling)* is a Dutch delicacy. A dish that harks back to the Calvinists is a basic meal of plaice *(schol)* with vegetables, where the fish is grilled and served with butter. You'll also find freshwater fish, called 'sweetwater fish' *(zoetwatervis)* by the Dutch, from some canals and rivers.

Smoked eel is a delicacy

Another favourite is herring *(haring)*, a small Atlantic fish that swims close to the North Sea shores. It is eaten raw. The typical Dutch way to eat herring is to take the tail in one hand, hold it above your mouth and slowly eat it in bites, so that the herring gradually disappears and only the tail is left. Amsterdammers often prefer herring chopped and served with raw chopped onions.

Herring from a street stall

CHEESE

Cheese *(kaas)* is eaten more often at breakfast or lunch rather than with dinner. Both Gouda and Edam, named after the towns where they are produced, are easily identifiable, being round in shape and covered in red (for export) or yellow wax that keeps the cheese airtight, allowing it to be kept for many months. Cheese fans should head for Reypenaer (www.reypenaercheese.com) in the centre of old Amsterdam with hour-long cheese-tasting sessions at least twice a day.

DESSERTS

The Dutch aren't known for their sweet tooth, although most cafés and restaurants will have *appelgebak* (apple pie) on the menu. You will also find *stroopwafels*, thin round waffles filled with golden syrup and butter; and *poffertjes*, small, shell-shaped pieces of dough, fried until brown in butter and sugar.

INDONESIAN CUISINE

The expansion of Dutch interests in the Golden Age brought a wealth of new ingredients and flavourings from the Far East. This added interest to native dishes, such as the Dutch habit of sprinkling nutmeg on cooked vegetables, but also, over the centuries, close ties with what is now Indonesia created a second Dutch national dish – *rijsttafel* (literally translated as 'rice table'). There are numerous Indonesian restaurants throughout the city offering *rijsttafel* with 10, 15 or 20 dishes. If you don't want a full *rijsttafel*, order *nasi rames*, a smaller selection of dishes served with rice – an ideal choice for lunch.

Rijsttafel is a Dutch invention, an interpretation of Indonesian cuisine – though often less spicy than the real thing – which became accepted both in the old colonies and in the Netherlands as a meal in itself. It consists of a number of small spicy meat, fish or vegetable dishes – up to 32 in total – and a communal serving of rice. Take a serving of rice and put it in the middle of your plate, then take small

Traditional brown café

amounts of the spicy dishes and place them around the outside of the rice. The small courses balance one another in taste, texture and heat (spiciness) to excite the palate.

The standard dishes include *babi* (pork), *daging bronkos* (roast meat in coconut milk), *goreng kering* (pimento and fish paste) and small skewers of meat (*satay*) with peanut sauce. Any dish that is labelled *sambal* is guaranteed to be

Cheese is eaten for breakfast or lunch in the Netherlands

hot (spicy), but hot dishes will be tempered with cooling ones such as marinated fruits and vegetables.

FOOD OF THE WORLD

Wander along just a few of Amsterdam's streets and it will soon become apparent that choice is the name of the game when it comes to eating out. If you want the best in French cuisine you will not be disappointed. Japanese restaurants abound for the very best in *sushi* or *teppanyaki*. Even good old steak can be found in Argentine, American and Mexican style.

Other European cuisines on offer are found in Spanish tapas bars and Greek tavernas – and you need look only a little further afield to find Egyptian kitchens, Moroccan *couscous* houses and South African bistros. All these are in addition to a fine selection of Italian, Chinese and Pan-Asian restaurants.

WHAT TO DRINK

The Dutch love their bars. You'll find one on almost every street corner; they are warm, welcoming places where you can sit for hours. The staple place to socialise is the *bruine kroeg* (brown café), as much an institution as the pub is in Britain. So called because of their brown-stained walls, low lighting and smoky interiors, brown bars sell alcohol, coffee and light snacks (see page 96).

Traditional Dutch bars have historically centred on two products. Beer is one and *jenever* (pronounced 'yen-eyfer')

CUTS IN THE COFFEE SHOPS

In Amsterdam, so-called 'coffee shops' have sold cannabis under a quasi-legal status for more than three decades. Their presence is tolerated largely because they segregate the users of soft drugs from the dealers who peddle harder substances.

There are around 150 establishments in the city where customers are able to sit back and indulge without suffering the paranoia of the wrong-doer.

The national coalition government elected in 2010 announced its intention to force the country's coffee shops to become private clubs, with membership available only to residents of the Netherlands. The ban came into effect in three southern provinces in May 2012; but six months later the new more liberal government shelved the law and left city authorities to decide whether to apply it or not. Amsterdam is in the process of closing a third of its 76 coffee shops (see page 33) but continues to allow tourists to purchase cannabis in those that remain open. Although cannabis is technically illegal in the Netherlands, coffee shops are allowed to sell up to 5 grams to anyone over 18. Visitors should be aware of the strength of local soft drugs and ask staff if in doubt.

the other. At one time, distillers and brewers had tasting houses (proeflokalen) for their products where buyers would convene to test the latest brews or compare vintages. Today, there are only a few of these remaining in the city and they always serve a range of other drinks, in addition to their traditional one.

Drinking jenever

De Drie Fleschjes (The Three Bottles) on Gravenstraat (behind Nieuwe Kerk) is the major *jenever* tasting house in the city, and has changed little in appearance since it was opened in 1650. Here you will be able to try different types of *jenever*. The young (jonge) clear *jenever* can be rather harsh to the palate, while the old (oude), aged in wooden casks, which impart a slightly yellow colour, is more mellow. There are also varieties of fruit-flavoured *jenever* to try.

In de Wildeman (www.indewildeman.nl) on Kolksteeg is a tasting house for beers, and its minimalist wood-panelled rooms impart something of the feeling of a religious experience to this drink, which has been so much a part of Amsterdam life since the 13th century. There are more than 50 types of beer available on draught, supplemented by nearly 100 different bottled beers. Dutch-produced beer is generally a pils variety, slightly stronger than British lager or American beer. If you order beer by the glass it will usually come in a 33cl (12fl oz) measure, served chilled. The two fingers of froth that crown your beer are traditional;

Double Dutch cheer

they are levelled with the top of the glass with a white plastic spatula. Heineken is the Netherlands' best-known beer and the former brewery has been converted into the Heineken Experience (www.heineken-experience.com) with light-hearted self-guided tours and a couple of free beers at the end.

As well as beer and *jenever*, most bars also serve wine, coffee and soft drinks. Coffee is the lifeblood of Amsterdam. The strong black short serving of fresh brew – and it must be fresh – is sold in cafés and bars all across the city.

TO HELP YOU ORDER

Could we have a table? **Heeft u een tafel voor ons?**
I'd like a/an/some... **Ik zou graag... willen hebben**

aperitif **een aperitief**	milk **melk**
beer **een bier**	mustard **mosterd**
butter **boter**	pepper **peper**
bread **brood**	potatoes **aardappels/ aardappelen**
coffee **koffie**	
dessert **een nagerecht**	rice **rijst**
fish **vis**	salad **sla**
fruit **fruit**	salt **zout**
meat **vlees**	sandwich **een boterham**
mineral water **mineraal water**	sugar **suiker**
	wine **wijn**

MENU READER

aardbeien strawberries	**kool** cabbage
ananas pineapple	**lamsvlees** lamb
biefstuk steak	friet French fries
bloemkool cauliflower	**perzik** peach
citroen lemon	**pruimen** plums
ei(eren) egg(s)	**rundvlees** beef
forel trout	**sinaasappel** orange
frambozen raspberries	**uien** onions
gehaktbal meatball	**uitsmijter** lunch snack of bread, ham and fried eggs
kaas cheese	
karbonade chop	**varkensvlees** pork
kersen cherries	**verse paling** fresh eel
kip chicken	**vrucht** fruit
kokosnoot coconut	**worst/worstje** sausage
konijn rabbit	

Out on the town in Amsterdam

PLACES TO EAT

*We have used the following symbols to give an idea
of the price for a three-course meal for one, including wine,
cover and service:*

€€€€ over 60 euros   €€€ 45-60 euros
€€ 30-45 euros   € below 30 euros

THE CENTRE

Hemelse Modder €€ *Oude Waal 11; tel: 020-624 3203,* www.
hemelsemodder.nl. A mixture of vegetarian and meat dishes with
French and Italian influences is served at this hip place along the
canal from the Montelbaanstoren. Daily 6pm–late.

In de Waag €€ *Nieuwmarkt 4; tel: 020-422 7772,* www.indewaag.
nl. The atmospheric setting of this bar/restaurant, in the Gothic
candlelit splendour of the old Weigh House with its huge beams,
would be enough to recommend it. The decor echoes this structure with huge tables for feasting. A mixed menu of fusion-style
dishes is served. Daily from 9am.

Nam Kee €€ *Zeedijk 111–13; tel: 020-624 3470.* This abidingly popular Chinese restaurant off Nieuwmarkt could double as Amsterdam's Chinatown all by itself, and it is still the heart of the district.
It eschews pretty much anything in the way of decor in favour of
authentic, no-frills Cantonese cuisine from an extensive menu.
Daily noon–11pm.

Gartine € *Taksteeg 7. tel: 020 320 4132,* www.gartine.nl. A hidden
gem off a small side street. The perfect place for breakfast and/
or light lunch, with a menu including croissants, jams, eggs Ben-
edict, pancakes, soups and salads. Brace yourself for long queues
at this popular joint.

Puccini Café € *Staalstraat 21; tel: 020-6208 458,* http://puccini.nl.
Great little café for breakfast, snack lunches or tea. Excellent
salads, soup and cakes – the chocolate truffle cake is hard to
resist as are the divine artisan chocolates in their sister shop,

Puccini Bonbon, nearby at no 17. Mon–Fri 8.30am–6pm, Sat–Sun 9am–6pm.

Restaurant Vermeer €€€€ *(in the NH Barbizon Palace Hotel) Prins Hendrikkade 59–72; tel: 020-556 4885,* www.restaurantvermeer.nl. One of the finest restaurants in Amsterdam, in a character-rich hotel facing Centraal Station. Serves a French menu with Dutch and Continental influences. Mon–Sat 6–10pm.

Il Pecorino €€ *Nordwal 1; tel: 020-737 1511,* www.ilpecorino.nl. You need to take a short, but free ferry trip from Centraal Station to enjoy this waterfront restaurant's rather short Italian menu including pastas, pizzas and a few other dishes. A fabulous, if often windswept, enclosed terrace affords a perfect viewpoint for observing the maritime comings and goings on the IJ waterway. Tue–Sun noon–9.30pm.

THE SOUTHEAST

Bord'Eau €€€€ *Hotel de l'Europe, Nieuwe Doelenstraat 2–14; tel: 020-531 1619,* http://bordeau.nl/. After a major revamp this elegant hotel restaurant with a prime location right on the River Amstel reopened and gained a Michelin star for its creative French cuisine. Each dish is a work of art. Tue–Fri noon–2pm, 6.30–10pm, Sat 6.30–10pm.

Dynasty €€€ *Reguliersdwarsstraat 30; tel: 020-626 8400,* www.restaurantdynasty.nl/. This place close to Koningsplein offers a tempting choice of Thai, Vietnamese and Chinese dishes all conveniently under one roof. You can choose from the set menus or go à la carte to mix and match your meal from different countries. The colourful dining room has a ceiling covered in parasols. Mon–Sun 5.30–10.30pm.

Haesje Claes €€€ *Spuistraat 273-5; tel: 020-624 9998;* www.haesjeclaes.nl/. Close to Spui, this comfortable, old-fashioned restaurant is full of nooks and crannies decorated with Delftware and hanging lamps. There is a wide-ranging menu but traditional Dutch dishes (especially stews) and steaks are the specialities of the house. Daily noon–midnight (kitchen closes at 10pm).

Izakaya €€€€ *Albert Cuypstraat 2-6; tel: 020-305 3090*, www.izakaya-amsterdam.com. Come with well-lined pockets for this Japanese culinary experience in the chic Sir Albert Hotel. The dishes are made to be shared: think oysters in filo pastry with wasabi sauce and caviar, dim sum of scallops with truffle sauce and succulent beef from beer-drinking Japanese cows. Music in the evening. daily 10am–11pm.

Kantjil & de Tijger €€€ *Spuistraat 291–3; tel: 020-620 0994*; www.kantjil.nl. Some of the most authentic Indonesian food to be found in the city is served in a modern but soothing Art Deco-influenced dining room at Spui. There is a range of vegetarian dishes on the menu. Daily noon–11pm.

La Rive €€€€ *(in the InterContinental Amstel Amsterdam Hotel) Professor Tulpplein 1; tel: 020-520 3264*, www.restaurantlarive.nl/. This formal French restaurant overlooking the River Amstel offers a polished gastronomic experience (it has a Michelin star). Excellent wine list. Reservations recommended. Daily 6.30–10pm.

Rose's Cantina €€ *Reguliersdwarsstraat 38–40; tel: 020-625 9797*. Busy Mexican restaurant behind the flower market, serving large portions of Tex-Mex cuisine, including enchiladas, tortillas, fajitas and sizzling chimichangas, plus a range of burgers. Pitchers of margarita are also available. Daily 9–midnight, until 5am Fri-Sat.

Sluizer €€€ *Utrechtsestraat 41–5; tel: 020-622 6376*, www.sluizer.nl. The plain wooden tables and simple but elegant decoration in this fish restaurant south of Rembrandtplein could grace any French bistro. There are two restaurants with a choice of excellent seafood – mussels a speciality – or French cuisine. Daily 5–11pm.

Tempo Doeloe €€€ *Utrechtsestraat 75; tel: 020-625 6718*; www.tempodoeloerestaurant.nl. One of the city's best Indonesian restaurants, with elegant decor. A too-enthusiastic embrace of the word *pedis* (hot) might bring tears to your eyes, but only a few dishes are so spicy they must be handled with care. Reservations essential. Mon–Sat 6pm–midnight.

Visrestaurant Lucius €€€ *Spuistraat 247; tel: 020-624 1831*, http://lucius.nl. Lucius, a block behind the flower market, specialises in seafood and fish dishes, ranging from huge plates of mussels to salmon and oysters. There is also a range of exotic species such as swordfish, and a limited choice for meat eaters. Good value set menu. Daily 5pm–midnight.

THE SOUTHWEST

De Blauwe Hollander €€ *Leidsekruisstraa 28, tel: 020-627 0521,* www.deblauwehollander.nl. Amid the international tourist-trap whirl around Leidseplein, this restaurant is a standard-bearer of traditional Dutch cuisine. If this seems like a dubious asset, be reassured that it does the business with a sense of style and a commitment to presenting the national menu in the best possible taste. Daily noon–11pm.

Le Garage €€€ *Ruysdaelstraat 54–6; tel: 020-679 7176,* http://restaurantlegarage.nl. This exciting bar/brasserie near the Rijksmuseum is owned by TV chef Joop Braakhekke. The atmosphere is bright and breezy and the food is French influenced. Mon–Fri noon–2pm, 6–11pm, Sat–Sun 6–11pm.

Wildschut €€ *Roelof Hartplein 1–3; tel: 020-676 8220,* http://cafe wildschut.nl. Set on a street corner a few blocks south of the Concertgebouw, with a pavement terrace that's among the city's most hallowed, this café-restaurant attracts a thirty-something yet still hip crowd that likes to see and be seen. Food ranges from moderately sophisticated bar snacks to well-prepared international dishes. Mon–Fri 9am–late, Sat–Sun 10am–late.

THE NORTHWEST

De Bolhoed €€ *Prinsengracht 60–2; tel: 020-626 1803.* With a great position beside the canal – and a tiny waterside terrace in summer – the 'Bowler Hat', housed in a former milliner's shop, adds a great location to a menu that brings zest to vegetarian and (for some dishes) vegan dining. The service is friendly and the soups, salads and inventive main courses add a spicy dimension to healthy eating. Daily 11am–midnight.

De Silveren Spiegel €€€€ *Kattengat 4–6; tel: 020-624 6589,* www. desilverenspiegel.com. You won't find a more typically Old Dutch-looking place than this. The menu is an updated version of classic Dutch cuisine, with added French influence for respectability. The five-course menu, paired with excellent wine, is widely praised and reasonably priced. Lovely atmosphere and friendly service. Mon –Sat 6–10pm.

De Vliegende Schotel € *Admiraal de Ruijterweg 331; tel: 06 8810 2129.* This Jordaan eatery serves some out-of-this-world veg-etarian and vegan cuisine. In the menu, there are international favourites including Spanish tortilla, Moroccan tagine with cous-cous and goulash. Freshly squeezed juices. Excellent selection of beers and wines. Daily noon–9.30pm.

La Oliva €€ *Egelantiersstraat 122-24; tel: 020-320 4316,* www.la oliva.nl. This Spanish wine bar in the heart of the Jordaan has a tempting array of early evening *pintxos* (Basque-style tapas) and an excellent choice of Spanish wines. Those with larger appetites can sit down to seafood starters, *pata negra* ham, fresh tuna or *zarzuela*, Catalan fish stew. Lunch menu (served until 4pm) is a good value. Mon–Sat noon-10pm.

Pancake Bakery € *Prinsengracht 191; tel: 020-625 1333,* www.pan cake.nl. Choose from around 70 different oversized Dutch pan-cakes, savoury or sweet, in this atmospheric warehouse close to Prinenstraat. The restaurant is located in a lovely 17th-cen-tury warehouse, which was once owned by the Dutch East India Company (VOC). The menu includes Mexican, Masai, Indonesian, Hungarian, Greek, French and even Greenlandic pancakes. Daily noon–9.30pm.

Yam Yam € *Frederik Hendrikstraat 88-90; 020 681 5097,* www.yam yam.nl. This trattoria is a favourite haunt of locals for its reason-ably priced stone-oven pizzas and fresh pasta. Tables spill out on to the terrace in the summer. It's nearly always full, so reserve a table or be prepared to queue. Affordable cocktails. Tue–Sun 5.30–11.30pm.

A–Z TRAVEL TIPS

A Summary of Practical Information

A

ACCOMMODATION (see also camping, youth hostels and the list of Recommended Hotels starting on page 133)

Amsterdam has a wide range of accommodation of all standards and prices, from über-cool new hotels to homely B&Bs. You can stay in a houseboat, a converted shipping container, or in a luxury suite at the top of a former industrial crane. Accommodation in the prime historic centre is limited and expensive, but cheaper hotels are popping up slightly further out, with good transport links. Hotels are rated from one to five stars. Prices are higher in summer. Service charge is included but the five percent city tourist tax may not be, so it is worth checking. Breakfast may also be an extra, ranging from €10–20 per person.

Given the architectural style of the buildings in Amsterdam you will find many of the lower-category hotels in the centre have steep, narrow staircases and no lift, so check before booking if you have problems climbing stairs or have young children. Also, many old houses have rooms of varying sizes and varying prices, so check this as well.

Amsterdam's tourist office website (www.iamsterdam.com) provides plenty of helpful information on accommodation and their tourist offices (see page 128) can also book a room (for a small fee) if you arrive without a reservation. This is not advisable during the summer or school holidays (exact dates vary but generally the end of May, the end of October, Easter and Christmas).

B&B rooms are also available, but not always with private facilities (Bed & Breakfast; tel: 040- 762 0600; www.bedandbreakfast.

I have a reservation. **Ik heb een reservering.**
What's the rate per night? **Hoeveel kost het per nacht?**

nl). Amsterdam House acts as an agent for a number of apartments and houseboats that can be rented short- or long-term. They can be contacted at 's-Gravelandse Veer 7, 1011 KM Amsterdam; tel: 020-624 6607; www.amsterdamhouse.com.

AIRPORT

Amsterdam Schiphol Airport (AMS; www.schiphol.nl), 18km (11 miles) southwest of the city centre, is one of the busiest and most modern airports in Europe. It acts as a gateway to Europe for airlines from around the world. Its tax-free shopping centre is considered among the best in the world.

There is a good rail connection from Schiphol Airport to Amsterdam Centraal Station. Trains run 24 hours a day, 5am–1am, every 10–15 minutes, otherwise hourly. The journey takes 20 minutes and costs €4.20. Tickets can be bought from machines with clear instructions in English and can be paid for with cash or credit card. You can also buy advance tickets online at www.discoverholland.com. Also available are one-day (€15), two-day (€20) and three-day (€25) travel cards, which provide the holder with unlimited travel on different means of public communication including train and Bus No 197 between airport and city.

Every 10–30 minutes from 6am–9.30pm a Connexxion Hotel Shuttle bus (tel: 038-339 4741; www.schipholhotelshuttle.nl) leaves the airport, stopping at many of the major hotels. Tickets (from €17 per person, the larger the group the lower the price per person) are sold at the Connexxion counter in the arrivals hall and on the bus. The bus will also take you back to the airport (return ticket costs €27). It is far cheaper to take Bus No 197/Amsterdam Airport Express, which takes half an hour and departs every 10 minutes between 5am and midnight, and costs €4.75 (€9 return) if bought on-line at www.bus197.nl. Otherwise, a single ticket costs €5. A taxi from the airport to the centre costs around €40–50.

B

BICYCLE HIRE *(fietsverhuur)*

Amsterdam is one of the most bicycle-friendly cities in the world, and cycling is a great way to get around. There are numerous places to hire bikes including MacBike (Stationsplein 5 at Centraal Station, Weteringschans 2 at Leidseplein and at Waterlooplein 199; tel: 020-620 0985; www.macbike.nl) and Rent-a-Bike Damstraat (Damsstraat 20–2, tel: 020-625 5029; www.bikes.nl). Rates begin at €10 a day for standard bikes with foot brakes (other types of bike are available). Cyclists are asked for ID, a cash deposit, or credit card details. Yellow Bike runs tours around the city and into the countryside (Nieuwezijds Kolk 29, tel: 020-620 6940; www.yellowbike.nl).

Riding a bike in a busy city is potentially risky. Take extra care and watch out for other road users. Amsterdammers don't wear crash helmets and bike-hire companies don't normally have them to hire. Always lock your bike, preferably against railings, and make sure you are fully insured.

I'd like to hire a bicycle. **Ik zou graag een fiets huren.**

BUDGETING FOR YOUR TRIP

Flights to Amsterdam. Prices from the UK vary hugely, starting at around £50 return on a low cost carrier in low season; scheduled return flights average £150.

Accommodation. Medium-quality double room for one night, €100–200.

Eating Out. Dish of the day in a cafe around €10–15, Indonesian *rijsttafel* €25 per person, three-course dinner for one excluding drinks: €35–45.

Transport passes. A day-pass valid on all forms of public transport is €15; two-day €20; three-day €25. Visit Amsterdam (www.iamster

dam.com) cards including free transport across the city 9 (excluding to/from the airport), free canal cruises, free entry to best museums and attractions as well as numerous discounts throughout Amsterdam cost €55 (one day), €65 (two days), €75 (three days), €85 (four days).

Entrance to museums. €5–17.50. To save on admissions, buy one of the museum cards: Visit Amsterdam (see above), the annual Museumkaart or Museumplein ticket (www.stedelijk.nl) which also gives free entry to any concert at the excellent Concertgebouw. All cards offer fast-lane entry to the museums.

Canal cruise. 75 minutes €16; dinner cruise from €80.

Check the Last-Minute Ticket Shop (www.lastminuteticketshop.nl) for half price seats at many events on the same day. The Concertgebouw (www.concertgebouw.nl) has free lunchtime concerts on Wednesday at 12.30pm from mid-September until late June. Vondelpark has free concerts and entertainment throughout the summer.

C

CAMPING

There are a number of campsites within a few minutes' journey from the city centre. They are well run and open all summer although they can fill up early, so it is sensible to make a reservation. Camping Het Amsterdamse Bos is in the large park area to the south of the city with a direct bus link to Centraal Station (tel: 020-641 6868; www.campingamsterdamsebos.nl). Camping Vliegenbos is north across the IJ waterway in 25 hectares (60 acres) of woods (tel: 020-636 8855; www.vliegenbos.com).

CAR HIRE

Amsterdam is a compact city with exceptionally good public transport and roads that favour bicycles. Parking is expensive and difficult to find. If you are planning to stay in the city, it is unlikely to be worth renting a car, but for touring the countryside it would certainly be worthwhile.

Most of the major international firms are represented in Amsterdam, and you will also find agencies at Schiphol airport.

Budget. tel: 088-284-7500; www.budget.nl
Europcar. tel: 020-316 4190; www.europcar.nl
Hertz. tel: 020-502 0240; www.hertz.nl
Sixt. tel: 020-405 9090; www.sixt.nl

Drivers must be over-21 (23 for some agencies) and have held a full licence for at least 12 months. National or international licences must be shown at the time of renting. Collision damage waiver is available at extra cost but is well worth the peace of mind – but do check your own vehicle, household or credit-card insurance, as you may already be covered.

I'd like to hire a car **Ik zou graag een auto willen huren**
today/tomorrow **vandaag/morgen**
for one day/a week **voor één dag/één week**
Please include full insurance. **Met een all-risk verzekering, alstublieft.**

CLIMATE

The Netherlands has unpredictable weather patterns similar to those of Britain, characterised by cold, wet winters and warm, wet summers. You can, however, have wonderful sunny days at any time of year, and Amsterdammers always hope for long periods of bright, cold winter spells.

Figures shown below are averages for each month and can vary.

	J	F	M	A	M	J	J	A	S	O	N	D
°C	7	8	11	13	16	18	20	21	17	14	11	8
°F	45	46	52	55	61	64	68	70	63	57	52	46

CLOTHING

It's a good idea to take several different types of clothing, even if you are travelling in summer, when in theory it should be warm. A layering system is the best approach. Always take a rainproof outer layer, whenever you visit, and an umbrella. In winter, a thick coat or jacket will keep you warm in cold spells, when the wind can bite.

On warm summer days, shorts, T-shirts, light shirts and trousers or light dresses are ideal, but always carry an extra layer just in case, and take a light sweater or jacket for the evenings. Comfortable walking shoes are essential, whatever time of year you travel.

CRIME AND SAFETY (see also emergencies and police)

Statistically, Amsterdam is one of the safest cities in Europe yet certain types of crime persist, notably luggage theft and pickpocketing. Always keep an eye on your luggage, especially at the airport, on the airport train, Centraal Station, or going to and from your hotel. Never carry cash, credit cards or passports in back pockets or an open handbag. Carry them in a body belt or inside a pocket with a zip. Be especially watchful in crowded squares and in the Red Light District.

As far as personal safety is concerned, after dark, keep to well-lit major thoroughfares. Many Amsterdammers walk (or go by bicycle) to social engagements, so unless you are very late you will be walking on streets with other people. If in doubt, get a tram – they run until just before midnight, and some have special night services. Otherwise, take a taxi.

A word on drugs: despite a relaxed attitude to (officially illegal, but tolerated) soft drugs, the possession of hard drugs is a criminal offence.

D

DRIVING

Driving within Amsterdam is not recommended. Streetside and canalside parking is expensive and difficult to find, and the excellent transport system precludes the need for your own car. There are very reasonably-priced Park & Ride parking lots off the A10 ring road, where you can leave your car for a maximum of four days.

Outside the city and throughout the Netherlands, road conditions are generally good. Vehicles are driven on the right. At roundabouts, give way to traffic from the right (unless signs indicate otherwise).

Speed limits. In towns or built up areas: 30 or 50kmh (20 or 30mph). On motorways: 120–130kmh (75mph), 100kmh on expressways, 80kmh (50mph) on regional roads. Other limits may be posted.

If you travel to Holland in your own car, you will need to carry your driving licence, registration document, or document of ownership, valid insurance, a red warning triangle in case of breakdown, and an international country identification sticker on the back of the car.

Parking. Tickets are dispensed from machines found every 100m (109yds) or so along streets and canals. Wardens are always on the lookout but cars are no longer clamped. There are large parking garages at various signposted locations around the city centre, open 24 hours a day. Parking in the city centre costs from around €5 per hour and up to €50 for a whole day. You can pay by credit card in these garages.

Fuel. Petrol stations are plentiful.

Assistance. If you need help, the anwb (Dutch Automobile Association; tel: 088-269 2888; www.anwb.nl) offers roadside assistance. If you hire a car, make sure you know what to do if you break down.

---

doorgaand verkeer through traffic
eenrichtingsverkeer one-way traffic
fietsers cyclists
gevaarlijke bocht dangerous bend
inhaalverbod no overtaking (passing)
let op... watch out for...

omleiding diversion (detour)
parkeerverbod no parking
pas op attention
rechts houden keep right
slecht wegdek bad road surface
snelheid verminderen reduce speed
uitrit exit
verboden in te rijden no entry for vehicles
verkeer over één rijbaan single-lane traffic
voetgangers pedestrians
wegomlegging diversion
werk in uitvoering roadworks in progress
(internationaal) rijbewijs (international) driving licence
kentekenbewijs car registration papers
groene kaart green card (insurance)

E

ELECTRICITY

The Netherlands operates on 230-volt/50-cycle current. Visitors from the UK or USA need an adapter for appliances. The better hotels may supply you with one, but they are easy to buy before you leave home. American 110-volt appliances require a transformer.

EMBASSIES AND CONSULATES

Although Amsterdam is the capital of the Netherlands, the diplomatic and political centre is Den Haag (The Hague) and all foreign embassies have their offices there.

Australia: Carnegielaan 4, 2517 KH Den Haag; tel: 070-310 8200; www.netherlands.embassy.gov.au.

Canada: Sophialaan 7, 2514 JP Den Haag; tel: 070-311 1600; www.canada.nl.

New Zealand: Eisenhowerlaan 77N, 2517 KK Den Haag; tel: 070-346 9324; www.mfat.govt.nz.
Republic of Ireland: Scheveningseweg 112, 2584 AE Den Haag; tel: 070-363 0993; www.dfa.ie/irish-embassy/the-netherlands/.
South Africa: Wassenaarseweg 40, 2596 CJ Den Haag; tel: 070-392 4501; www.zuidafrika.nl.
UK: Lange Voorhout 10, 2514 ED Den Haag; tel: 070-427 0427; www.gov.uk.
US: Lange Voorhout 102, 2514 EJ Den Haag; tel: 070-310 2209; http://thehague.usembassy.gov.
Consulates in Amsterdam
UK: Koningslaan 44; tel: 070-427 0427; www.gov.uk.
US: Museumplein 19; tel: 020-575 5309; http://amsterdam.usconsulate.gov.

EMERGENCIES (see also police)

For emergencies (fire, police or ambulance) dial **112**.
If you are a victim of crime go to a police station (see page 125).

(see page 125)

G

GAY AND LESBIAN TRAVELLERS

Amsterdam is an extremely friendly city for gay and lesbian visitors. Gay Pride in early August is one of the world's largest gay celebrations, drawing over 350,000 participants. There are hotels that cater specifically for gays and a vibrant social scene. The website of the Gay Tourist Information Centre (GAYtic) at Spuistraat 44 (www.gaytic.nl) is packed with useful information, as is www.nighttours.com, a travel guide to the city's gay life.

GETTING THERE

By air. Most of the world's major airlines operate flights to Amsterdam Airport Schiphol, and KLM (www.klm.com), the national airline of the Netherlands, has a large network and flies from the UK, US, Canada, South Africa, Australia and New Zealand.

There are several flights to Schiphol daily from London airports, Manchester and other regional UK airports. Flights from London take under an hour. British Airways (tel: 0844-493 0787; www.ba.com) flybe (www.flybe.com), easyJet (www.easyjet.com) and KLM all operate services. Aer Lingus (www.aerlingus.com) has a regular service to Amsterdam from Dublin.

Other airlines that run nonstop services to Schiphol include Delta (www.delta.com) and United (www.united.com).

By sea. P&O Ferries operates a daily service from Hull to Rotterdam (tel: 0800 130 0030; www.poferries.com). Stena Line (tel: 08447-770 7070; www.stenaline.co.uk) sails from Harwich to Hoek van Holland. DFDS Seaways (tel: 0871-522 9955; www.dfdsseaways.co.uk) from Newcastle to Amsterdam.

By rail. Eurostar (tel: 08432 186 186; www.eurostar.com) in cooperation with Dutch Railways is planning to launch a direct service between London and Amsterdam from late 2017. The journey time will be around four hours. Until then, travellers from Britain can use the Eurostar service from London through the Channel Tunnel to Brussels, and onward from there by high-speed Thalys train.

By road. Going by coach is cheap but takes 12 hours. Eurolines (tel: 0871-781 8177; www.eurolines.co.uk) run up to three buses a day from London to Amsterdam. By car, you can either take one of the car ferry services above, or ferries that sail to ports in Belgium and France; or put your car on a Eurotunnel shuttle train (tel: 08443 353 535; www.eurotunnel.com).

GUIDES AND TOURS

There are a number of qualified English-speaking guides who offer tours of the city. Some have specialities; some take groups or offer an individual service. Contact the tourist information office (see page 128) for a list.

A number of companies offer boat tours along the canals and these are probably the most popular activities in the city. Multilingual commentary keeps you informed about the attractions as you float along past them. Contact Rederij Lovers (tel: 020-530 1090; www.lovers.nl) or simply head to Damrak and Stationsplein and other docks from where the boats depart.

Yellow Bike offers accompanied bike tours of the city with English-speaking guides (tel: 020-620 6940; www. yellowbike. nl).

H

HEALTH AND MEDICAL CARE

The Netherlands is a modern, well-run country, and its medical facilities are excellent. There are no health concerns, although mosquitoes can be a nuisance in the summer, so anti-mosquito sprays or creams are useful. You will not need inoculations and the water is safe to drink. Most doctors and other medical professionals speak English. Always take out suitable travel insurance to cover any health problem you may have on your trip. You will be asked to pay for some medical treatment and should cover yourself against something serious happening to you. If you are an EU citizen, you will be covered for medical treatment by participating doctors/hospitals if you have a European Health Insurance Card (ehic), available online at www.ehic.org.uk. You will need to pay for treatment at the time but will be able to claim a refund on return.

Many proprietary brands of drugs are available over the counter from any pharmacy *(apotheek)*. A trained pharmacist will be able to give sound advice about medicines for minor ailments. Call 694 8709 to find out which pharmacies are open after hours and for referral to local doctors and dentists.

L

LANGUAGE

There are around 30 million speakers of Dutch in the world, with Afrikaans (South Africa) and Flemish (Vlaams) of Belgium being closely allied to it. Its structure is similar to German, but it is grammatically simpler. That said, the Dutch usually speak English very well (and other languages passably), so you will rarely need to resort to your language phrasebook. However, knowing and using a few words of the language of the country you are visiting is only polite, and it may gain you some friendly comments.

Do you speak English? **Spreekt u Engels?**
What does this mean? **Wat betekent dit?**
I don't understand **Ik begrijp het niet**
Good morning **Goede morgen**
Good afternoon **Goede middag**
Good evening **Goeden avond**
Please/Thank you **Alstublieft/Dank u**
You're welcome **Alstublieft/Graag gedaan**

M

MAPS

The Tourist Office or VVV (see page 128) produces a city map for a small charge, with museums, sights and public transport. For more detail opt for the Falk Map of Amsterdam (1:15,000), also available to purchase at the VVV. The *Insight Fleximap to Amsterdam* is detailed and easy to use, with a full street index and a laminated finish that means the frequent Amsterdam rain is not a problem.

The Tourist Guide to Public Transport in Amsterdam has a map with public transport services superimposed on the basic city map.

MEDIA

Newspapers and magazines *(kranten, tijdschriften)*. Many English newspapers and magazines can be readily bought in the city. British daily papers are available soon after they are on sale at home. US papers will be a day old but the *International Herald Tribune* is published daily in Paris, so is on sale on the same day it is published. Several tourist information magazines in English are available, either for a charge at newsstands or free at many hotels. The best is A-mag, published by the tourist board every two months and providing lively sections on what to do and see in the city.

TV and radio *(televisie, radio)*. There are a number of Dutch television stations mainly serving the local community and sometimes taking services from various European countries, including British stations. The Dutch use subtitles to translate foreign programmes, rather than dubbing, so you will be able to understand the broadcasts – this is one of the reasons why the Dutch are so adept at speaking English and other languages. Most major hotels offer CNN and the BBC in your room.

In most places in the Netherlands you should be able to get good reception for BBC radio transmissions.

MONEY

In common with most other EU countries, the euro (€) is used in the Netherlands. Notes are denominated in 5, 10, 20, 50, 100, 200 and 500 euros; coins in 1 and 2 euros and 1, 2, 5, 10, 20 and 50 cents.

Currency can be exchanged in banks and bureaux de change offices, which can be found at Centraal Station, in Leidseplein and in major shopping areas. These offices are open longer hours than banks. The gwk Travelex exchange office in Centraal Station, with branches at Leidseplein and Schiphol Airport, provides a good service. Banks normally offer the best rates. International ATMs are common and are indicated by the Cirrus or Plus signs on the machine. Most hotels accept credit cards but it is not always the case with shops and restaurants.

I'd like to change some pounds/dollars. **Ik wil graag ponden/ dollars wisselen.**
Do you accept traveller's cheques? **Accepteert u reischeques?**
Can I pay with credit card? **Kan ik met deze credit card betalen?**

Major credit cards are widely accepted in hotels, restaurants and shops, although there may be a minimum limit on payments in shops.

O

OPENING TIMES (see also holidays)
Offices and most government offices are generally open Mon–Fri 9am–5pm. Most banks are open Mon–Fri 9am–5pm; late opening Thur from 4.30pm–7pm.

Shops are generally open Mon 1pm–6pm, Tue–Sat 9am–6pm, (until 9pm on Thur), Sun noon–5pm.

P

POLICE (see also emergencies)
The police headquarters (*hoofdbureau van de politie*) is at Elandsgracht 117; tel: 0900 8844. There is also a large police station at Lijnbaansgracht 219. The emergency number is 112.

Police wear navy-blue uniforms and carry firearms. They are approachable to answer basic questions such as giving directions.

POST OFFICES

All post offices in Amsterdam have closed apart from the central post office at Singel 250, open Mon–Fri 7.30am–6.30pm, Sat 7.30am–5pm. It is often busy, so avoid it if you only want to buy stamps, which are available at tobacconists and the majority of shops selling postcards.

A stamp for this letter/postcard, please **Een postzegel voor deze brief/briefkaart, alstublieft**
airmail **luchtpost**
registered **aangetekend**

PUBLIC HOLIDAYS

The following dates are official holidays:
1 January *Nieuwjaar* New Year's Day
27 April (or 26 if it falls on a Sunday) *Koninginnedag* King's Birthday
25–26 December *Kerst* Christmas
Moveable holidays are as follows:
Goede Vrijdag Good Friday
Tweede Paasdag Easter Monday
Hemelvaartsdag Ascension Day
Tweede Pinksterdag Whit Monday
All shops and offices are closed for all the above holidays.

T

TELEPHONES

The international code for the Netherlands is 31, and the city code for Amsterdam is 020. To call a number within the city use just the seven-digit number. To call an Amsterdam number from other parts of the Netherlands, dial 020 first. If dialling from outside the country dial your international country code + 31 20 and the seven-digit number.

Virtually all of the public phones around the city are out of use. If you happen to find one that is working you will need a credit card or a phonecard, available from newsagents and tobacconists.

Roaming is possible on Holland's tri-band and quad-band enabled GSM mobile-phone network. Phones to rent and purchase are widely available from phone stores, as are prepaid SIM cards for using your own (unlocked) phone at Dutch rates. Be sure to bring an appropriate plug adaptor and, if needed, a voltage transformer for charging your phone.

TIME ZONES

The Netherlands is one hour ahead of Greenwich Mean Time (GMT). From the last weekend in March to the last weekend in October, the clocks are advanced one hour – this change corresponds with the rest of the EU. During the European summer, the time differences are:

New York	London	**Amsterdam**	Jo'burg	Sydney	Auckland
6am	11am	**noon**	noon	8pm	10pm

TIPPING

Service charges are included in all bar, restaurant and hotel bills. However, an extra tip to show gratitude for good service is always appreciated. It is appropriate to leave the small change on the table in bars and cafés.

The following situations are still discretionary:

Taxi fares: round up the fare.

Hotel porter: €1–2 per bag.

Tour guide: 10–15 percent.

Concierge: discretionary according to services provided.

TOILETS

There are few public toilet facilities in the city but department stores and the Magna Plaza mall have toilets, as do all the museums, and many of the city's top hotels have toilets just off the lobby. Bars and cafés are designated public places, but it is considered polite to have a drink if you use their facilities. Toilets for females may be indicated with the word Dames, and those for males with *Heren*.

Where is the toilet? **Waar is het toilet?**

TOURIST INFORMATION

The all-embracing Amsterdam tourist office website (www.i amsterdam.com) is likely to cover all your queries but should you need information on other parts of the Netherlands go to the official Holland website: www.holland.com.

In Amsterdam

For information, maps, hotel bookings and tickets, visit the VVV tourist office (tel: 020-702 6000; www.iamsterdam.com) at Stationsplein 10, opposite the entrance to Centraal Station, daily 9am–6pm. Take a ticket when you arrive and expect a long wait. Staff can arrange hotel accommodation (for a small fee), book theatre and museum tickets, sell you the I Amsterdam discount card and provide a city map (for a small charge). There is also a Visitor information centre at Centraal station (Mon–Wed 9am–6pm, Thu–Sat 9am–8pm, Sun 9am–6pm) and at Schiphol Airport (daily 7am–10pm), which is useful if you have not booked accommodation.

TRANSPORT

Public transport in Amsterdam is excellent. The GVB (tel: 0900-8011; www.gvb.nl) municipal transport company runs a comprehensive network of trams, buses, trains, metro and boats. The ferries are free. Information, route maps, timetables and public transport passes are available from the GVB Tickets & Info office on Stationsplein, outside Centraal Station.

OV-chipkaart. In Amsterdam and throughout the Netherlands, journeys for the trams, buses and metro are paid for with a public transport card, the credit card-size OV-chipkaart. 'OV' stands for Openbaar Vervoer (public transport). The most convenient option for visitors are the one-hour cards or (multi)-day cards available from the conductor on buses and trams, at GVB ticket vending machines or information locations, or an anonymous card that can be purchased or topped up with credit at newsstands and supermarkets as well as GVB ticket vending machines and information offices.

Travel passes. Depending on your travel plans and the duration of your stay these can provide one of the most affordable ways of travelling by public transport. Your pass allows you to travel on any form of public transport at any time for the duration of the pass. There are one to seven day passes starting from €7.50, but for more days it becomes even better value. For details and other options see www.iamsterdam.com or http://en.gvb.nl.

Drivers and conductors also sell 1-hour (€2.90) and 24-hour (€7.50) disposable cards on trams and buses. Remember to check in and check out on every journey at one of the card readers. Cards are valid nationwide. Reduced-rate cards are available for seniors and children.

Don't forget about the one, two or three-day I amsterdam City Card (see page 27), which allows free entry to most museums and free transport in the city. Cards are available from VVV offices and at the gvb ticket office opposite Centraal Station.

Trams. Amsterdam has an excellent network of trams. Many tram stops are in the middle of the road, with traffic passing on both sides – take care when getting on and off, and keep young children close to you; if a tram has a conductor you must enter at or towards the rear, otherwise enter by any door. Press one of the bells found at regular intervals along the carriage to get off at the next stop.

Bus. An extensive bus network operated by the GVB (see page 128), and by regional operators like Connexxion (www.connexxion.nl) and Arriva (www.arriva.nl), go to places the trams might not reach, but the tram network is generally the best way to get around. After midnight when trams stop, a night bus network is in operation. Like the trams, only one-hour tickets can be purchased on-board, other types of tickets can be bought at GVB Ticket and information offices or GVB ticket vending machines.

Metro. The Amsterdam metro currently has four lines designed to link the city centre with the suburbs and as such are not as useful as other forms of public transport for visiting tourist attractions. A controversial new line is currently under construction to link the south of the city with the north.However, major delays have been caused by damage to the foundations of several historic buildings and spiralling costs. Originally due for completion in 2011, the line will not be complete until at least 2017.

Water buses. The Museum Line boats run along the canals between the major city sights at 45-minute intervals. Day tickets cost €27.50 for 24 hoursavailable from the Rederij Lovers ticket office (tel: 020-530 1090; www.lovers.nl) opposite Centraal Station. Canal Bus (tel: 020-217 0500; www.canal.nl) boats operate on four separate routes through the canals and offer day cruises, cocktail and dinner cruises.

Ferry GVB ferries transport passengers (and their bikes and mopeds) from Centraal Station across the River IJ to various locations in Amsterdam Noord iver IJ t completely free of charge.

Taxis can be found at ranks across the city, including Centraal Station, the Dam and Leidseplein. Officially you are not allowed to flag them down in the street but it is always worth a try. Regulated fares have been introduced: the maximum start price is €2.83, maximum price per kilometre €2.08.

Water taxis. Not for budget travellers, costing €50 per half hour in the city centre, but the boats hold eight people. Contact Watertaxi at Stationsplein 8; tel: 020-535 6363.

TRAVELLERS WITH DISABILITIES

With its cobbled streets, narrow canal house stairways and inaccessible trams, Amsterdam may present challenges to travellers with mobility problems. However most museums, attractions and public buildings are accessible to wheelchair users, some of the canal cruise operators use wheelchair lifts and a few of the taxis offer access.

A useful source of information and advice is Tourism for All, tel: 0845-124 9971, www.tourismforall.org.uk.

V

VISAS AND ENTRY REQUIREMENTS

Citizens of the EU, US, Australia and New Zealand can visit for up to three months on production of a valid passport. South African citizens need a visa.

EU residents can import or export unlimited amounts of goods for personal use, on which duty has been paid, although guidelines for personal use are as follows: 800 cigarettes, 400 cigars or cigarillos, 1kg tobacco, 10 litres of spirits, 90 litres of wine, 110 litres of beer.

Non-EU nationals or EU citizens travelling from non-EU countries can import tax-free goods to the following limits: 200 cigarettes or 50 cigars or 100 cigarillos, or 250g of tobacco, 1 litre of spirits or 2 litres of fortified or sparkling wine, 4 litres of still wine, 16 litres of beer and other goods including gifts up to the value of €500.

Non-EU residents can receive a refund of up to 21 percent on goods purchased in certain shops to take home. To qualify for a refund you must spend more than €50 in one shop in one day, and the goods must be exported within three months. You must have the purchases, receipt and the refund cheque available for customs officials to view as you leave the country For further information contact www.vatfree.com.

W

WEBSITES AND INTERNET ACCESS

Many city hotels, along with some cafés, bars, coffee houses and other locations offer free or paid-for Wi-fi internet access and have a terminal or terminals in the lobby. Free WiFi is also available at Schipol airport.

The following websites are useful for trip planning:

www.iamsterdam.com is the VVV Amsterdam's own comprehensive website, with lots of travel information and news on the city's attractions.

www.holland.com has a comprehensive information on all regions and major cities in the country as well as useful practical information section.

www.amsterdamhotspots.nl As its name suggests, this covers the hottest places for eating, drinking, dancing and much more.

www.iens.nl Comprehensive dining out website, with reader reviews in both English and Dutch.

Y

YOUTH HOSTELS

There are a number of youth hostels in the city. For more information, contact the Dutch youth hostel association, Stayokay; www.stayokay. com. Stayokay hostels offer discounts to members of the International Youth Hostel Association. Amsterdam's main one, Stayokay Amsterdam Vondelpark, with 540 beds, is at Vondelpark (Zandpad 5; tel: 020-589 8996; www.stayokay.com). For more noise and action try Hostel Amsterdam Stadsdoelen (see page 134). Reservations for all youth hostels are recommended at peak times and most weekends.

RECOMMENDED HOTELS

The Netherlands Board of Tourism has rated more than 200 recommended hotels in the city, but there are also many unclassified establishments, which represent good value.

Prices are high by international standards but quality is usually high too. A number of new hotels have sprouted outside the main canal ring, with cheaper prices and good transport to the centre.

The following price categories are for one night in high season for two people in a double room with private facilities, including breakfast. Most large hotels charge five percent city tax in addition to the room price; smaller hotels may include the tax in the price. Some hotels include breakfast in the price, although an increasing number, especially in the four and five star category charge for breakfast separately.

€€€€	250–500 euros
€€€	140–250 euros
€€	90–140 euros
€	below 90 euros

THE CENTRE

Mövenpick Hotel Amsterdam City Centre €€€ *Piet Heinkade 11, 1019 BR Amsterdam; tel: 020-519 1200; www.moevenpick-hotels. com/amsterdam.* What you see is clearly what you get at this huge, high-rise modern hotel, overlooking the IJ waterway just east of Centraal Station – the most stunning harbour views in Amsterdam, and all the tried-and-tested virtues of a stellar branch of the Swiss chain.

NH Barbizon Palace €€€€ *Prins Hendrikkade 59–72, 1012 AD Amsterdam; tel: 020-556 4564; www.nh-hotels.com.* A large five-star hotel, next to the Sint-Nicolaaskerk and opposite Centraal Station, which combines old canal houses with a modern entrance and reception area. There are several restaurants, including the highly regarded Vermeer (see page 107).

Rho €€ *Nes 5–23, 1012 KC Amsterdam; tel: 020-620 7371;* www.rho hotel.com. A good-value hotel located on a quiet street one block back from Rokin. The building was once a theatre and retains several original features from that time. Rooms are modern in style.

Sofitel Amsterdam The Grand €€€€ *Oudezijds Voorburgwal 197, 1012 EX Amsterdam; tel: 020-555 3111;* www.sofitel-legend-thegrand. com. Built in 1578 as a Royal Inn, this building became Amsterdam City Hall following the loss of the Palace on the Dam and is situated in the heart of the old city. The exterior is an historic monument while the interior has been refurbished to an extremely high standard. There are excellent spa facilities (at extra cost) for guests.

Winston Amsterdam Hostel € *Warmoesstraat 129, 1012 JA Amsterdam; tel: 020-623 1380;* www.winston.nl. Borderline-grungy, as befits an establishment bordering the Red Light District, the hotel and hostel rambles through a large building with pretensions to an arthouse style, attracting a mostly youthful clientele with bustle, a beer garden and an up-to-the-minute dance club.

THE SOUTHEAST

Hotel de l'Europe €€€€ *Nieuwe Doelenstraat 2–14, 1012 CP Amsterdam; tel: 020-531 1777;* www.leurope.nl. Justifiably regarded as one of the city's premier lodgings, this centrally located hotel is housed in a building dating from 1896, but beautifully renovated to offer five-star luxury accommodation. It stands on the banks of the Amstel, where the river flows into the canals.

InterContinental Amstel Amsterdam €€€€ *Professor Tulpplein 1, 1018 GX, Amsterdam; tel: 020-622 6060;* www.amsterdam.intercontin ental.com/en. The 'grande dame' of Amsterdam hotels occupies a prime location on the east bank of the River Amstel. Exquisite interiors define a mid-size establishment favoured by international stars, top politicians, and leading business people.

Prinsenhof €€ *Prinsengracht 810, 1017 JL Amsterdam; tel: 020-623 1772;* www.hotelprinsenhof.com. This hotel offers budget travellers a chance to experience life in an Amsterdam canal house in a central location. The beamed rooms are bright, clean and thoughtfully furnished. Breakfasting with a view of the Prinsengracht is a definite plus.

Seven Bridges €€€ *Reguliersgracht 31, 1017 LK Amsterdam; tel: 020-623 1329;* www.sevenbridgeshotel.nl. Sitting on one of the prettiest canals, this is among the most individual hotels in the city, with stylishly furnished rooms, stripped floorboards, oriental rugs and elegant antiques. There are no public rooms, so breakfast is served in your room.

THE SOUTHWEST

Hampshire Hotel American Amsterdam€€€ *Leidsekade 97, 1017 PN Amsterdam; tel: 035 677 7217;* www.hampshirehotelamsterdamamerican.com. Set amid the bars, restaurants and clubs of Leidseplein, this Art Deco hotel favoured by celebrities and pop stars, and is a designated historic monument. The sound-proofing does a great job of cutting off the considerable noise that emanates after dark from the many bars and cafés nearby and sometimes keeps going way into the night.

Andaz Amsterdam €€€€ *Prinsengracht 587; tel: 021-523 1234;* www.amsterdamprinsengracht.andaz.hyatt.com. Leading Dutch interior designer Marcel Wanders, renowned for his flamboyant interiors, has transformed what was a dreary public library into a chic hotel. Decor is playful and surreal, the atmosphere cool and the bedrooms luxurious.

Apple Inn €€ *Koninginneweg 93, 1075 CJ Amsterdam; tel: 020-662 7894,* www.apple-inn.nl. A place that looks as fresh as a just-picked fruit, this smallish hotel fills its elegant 19th-century town house just off Vondelpark with light, and features pastel-shaded decor, rooms that emphasise comfort and integrated design, and there's a garden at the rear.

Best Western Apollo Museumhotel Amsterdam City Centre €€€ *P.C. Hooftstraat 2, 1071 BX Amsterdam; tel: 020-662 1402;* www.bestwestern.com. Just off Museumplein and Leidseplein, this good-value option for independent travellers has modern and comfortable – if not particularly distinguished – rooms, but scores highly for location.

Conscious Hotel Museum Square €€€ *De Lairessestraat 7, 1071 NR Amsterdam; tel: 020-671 9596;* www.conscioushotels.com. Part of the Conscious Hotels, this small eco-design hotel opposite the Concertgebouw, has fresh bright rooms and contemporary hip decor. Very handy for Museumplein.

Conservatorium €€€€ *Van Baerlestraat 27; tel: 020-570 0000;* www. conservatoriumhotel.com. Opened in 2011, this see-and-be-seen-in 5-star hotel was converted from the Sweelinck Music Conservatory. It is a stunning blend of old and new, transformed by Italian architect and designer Piero Lissoni in chic contemporary style, while losing none of its former beauty.

Dikker & Thijs Fenice €€€ *Prinsengracht 444; tel: 020-620 1212;* www.dikkerandthijshotelamsterdam.com. Occupying a 20th century house and a converted warehouse on the Prinsengracht, the hotel has lovely views from its canalside rooms. There is not much in the way of public rooms but the classic-style guest rooms are a decent size and good value for a 4-star hotel. It's also in a great location – just around the corner from Leidseplein.

Mozart €€ *Prinsengracht 518–20, 1017 KJ Amsterdam; tel: 020-620 9546;* www.hotelmozart.nl. Close to Leidseplein, the Mozart is a modest but stalwart canal house hotel, squeezing decent modern furnishings and a few neat design touches into an old building's tight quarters, while regularly updating and striving to provide value for money.

Park Hotel €€€€ *Stadhouderskade 25, 1071 ZD Amsterdam; tel: 020-710 7277;* www.parkhotel.nl. Across the street from Leidseplein and only minutes from Museumplein, the Park is a fashionable boutique hotel in contemporary style. The trendy Momo restaurant wins awards for its Pan-Asian cuisine.

THE NORTHWEST

Ambassade €€€ *Herengracht 341, 1016 AZ Amsterdam; tel: 020-555 0222;* www.ambassade-hotel.nl. Ten historic canal houses within a few minutes' walk of the city centre have been amalgamated to create the delightful Ambassade. The hotel scores highly for stylish rooms and attentive, friendly staff.

Hotel IX €€€€ *Hartenstraat 8; tel: 020-845 8451;* www.hotelix amsterdam.com. In the heart of the old town, the IX is a brand new boutique hotel in the middle of the Negen Straatjes (9 streets) shopping district. Located in a fine 17th century building, it has five suites, with bathrooms, and free Wi-Fi throughout.

Best Western Dam Square Inn €€€ *Gravenstraat 12–16, 1012 NM Amsterdam; tel: 020-623 3716;* www.bestwestern.com. Housed in the building of an old distillery, this cosy hotel has a thoroughly modern interior. It is pleasant, quiet and friendly, and only minutes from the centre.

Die Port van Cleve €€€ *Nieuwezijds Voorburgwal 176–80, 1012 SJ Amsterdam; tel: 020-714 2000;* www.dieportvancleve.com. Just behind the Royal Palace, the hotel has an ornate facade and a historic bar with Delft tile decoration.

The Exchange €€€ *Damrak 50, tel: 020-523 0080;* www.hotelthe exchange.com. The owners of the successful Lloyd Hotel (see page 138) opened The Exchange in 2011, and it is one of the coolest spots to stay in the city. Creatively designed by graduates from the Amsterdam Fashion Institute, the 62 guest rooms range from 2–5 star: expect anything from Marie-Antoinette opulence to a room with a tent.

NH Grand Hotel Krasnapolsky €€€€ *Dam 9, 1012 JS Amsterdam; tel: 020-554 9111;* www.nh-hotels.com. An imposing hotel opposite the Royal Palace on the Dam. Rooms are all shapes and sizes, in different parts of a rambling complex. Several restaurants, and a pretty interior garden with an outdoor café terrace.

BEYOND THE CITY CENTRE

Amstel Botel € *NDSM-Pier 3, 1033 RG Amsterdam; tel: 020-626 4247;* www.amstelbotel.nl. The only floating hotel in the city, this converted river cruise boat, moored at the NDSM Wharf, a 15-minute free ferry trip from Centraal Station, offers compact modern cabin rooms, some with harbour views.

Arena €€ *'s-Gravesandestraat 51, 1092 AA Amsterdam; tel: 020-850 2400;* www.hotelarena.nl. Close to the Tropenmuseum in Amsterdam-Oost, the rambling Arena is an eclectic mix of superbly restored monumental buildings providing the setting for lodging, dining, drinking and dancing that appeals to independent travellers.

Dutch Design Hotel Artemis Amsterdam €€ *John M Keynesplein 2, 1066 EP Amsterdam; tel: 020-714 1001;* www.artemisamsterdam. com. The large, modern hotel in the leafy but undistinguished western Slotervaart district lives up to its design-focused billing, and that, together with a waterfront setting and a De Stijl-influenced restaurant, might easily win you over.

Jaz in the City Hotel €€ *De Passage 90, 1101 AX Amsterdam–Zuidoost, tel: 020 210 5800,* www.jaz-hotel.com. Situated across from the Amsterdam ArenA, this new hotel features 247 trendy and stylish rooms and 11 suites. Cool beats, sleek drinks and lounge atmosphere rule at the local Rhythms Bar & Kitchen. Also features a spa and fitness area.

Lloyd €€€ *Oostelijke Handelskade 34, 1019 BN Amsterdam; tel: 020-561 3607;* www.lloydhotel.com. An innovative hotel converted from a prison on the redeveloped harbour-side east of Centraal Station, the Lloyd has a well-deserved reputation as a cool place to stay, with artworks and cutting-edge fusion cuisine. Rooms are categorised from 1-5 star and priced accordingly.

INSIGHT ⊙ GUIDES POCKET GUIDE

AMSTERDAM

First Edition 2017

Editor: Tom Fleming
Author: Lindsey Bennett
Head of Production: Rebeka Davies
Picture Editor: Tom Smyth
Cartography Update: Carte
Update Production: AM Services
Photography Credits: Alamy 63; Allard
Bovenberg/AFF/AFHí 68; Bigstock 6ML, 74,
77, 79, 93, 98; Corbis 18, 22; DigiDaan/NEMO
Science Museum 5M; Dreamstime 7TC, 31, 32,
34, 35, 81, 97, 101; Fotolia 8L, 30, 36, 64, 85;
Getty Images 4TC, 4MC, 4ML, 5M, 26, 72; Glyn
Genin/Apa Publications 44, 47; Greg Gladman/
Apa Publications 5MC, 6TL, 6TL, 7M, 9R, 11,
13, 14, 28, 39, 45, 46, 49, 52, 53, 55, 66, 69,
89, 90, 94, 100, 103, 104, 105; iStock 6ML, 7T,
21, 24, 41, 51, 82, 99; Jan Kees Steenman/Van
Gogh Museum Amsterdam 59; JL Marshall/
Rijksmuseum 5MC, 56; JL Marshall/Stedelijk
Museum 6MC; Museum Willet-Holthuysen
8R, 43; NBTC 7M, 57, 70; Public domain 60;
Shutterstock 4TL, 5T, 9, 16, 67, 76, 78, 86, 87,
88; Vincent van Gogh Foundation 5TC
Cover Picture: Shutterstock

Distribution
UK, Ireland and Europe: Apa Publications
(UK) Ltd; sales@insightguides.com
United States and Canada: Ingram Publisher
Services; ips@ingramcontent.com
Australia and New Zealand: Woodslane;
info@woodslane.com.au
Southeast Asia: Apa Publications (SN) Pte;
singaporeoffice@insightguides.com

Hong Kong, Taiwan and China:
Apa Publications (HK) Ltd;
hongkongoffice@insightguides.com
Worldwide: Apa Publications (UK) Ltd;
sales@insightguides.com

**Special Sales, Content Licensing
and CoPublishing**
Insight Guides can be purchased in bulk
quantities at discounted prices. We can create
special editions, personalised jackets and
corporate imprints tailored to your needs.
sales@insightguides.com;
www.insightguides.biz

All Rights Reserved
© 2017 Apa Digital (CH) AG and
Apa Publications (UK) Ltd

Printed in China by CTPS

No part of this book may be reproduced,
stored in a retrieval system or transmitted in
any form or means electronic, mechanical,
photocopying, recording or otherwise,
without prior written permission from Apa
Publications.

Contact us
Every effort has been made to provide
accurate information in this publication,
but changes are inevitable. The publisher
cannot be responsible for any resulting loss,
inconvenience or injury. We would appreciate
it if readers would call our attention to any
errors or outdated information. We also
welcome your suggestions; please contact us
at: hello@insightguides.com
www.insightguides.com

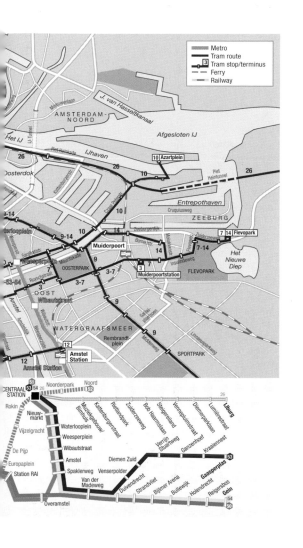